Pathway to Renewal

Practical Steps for Congregations

Pathway toRenewal

Practical Steps for Congregations

Daniel P. Smith
and Mary K. Sellon

THE
ALBAN
INSTITUTE

Herndon, Virginia
www.alban.org

The Alban Institute
2121 Cooperative Way, Suite 100
Herndon, VA 20171

Unless otherwise noted, all Scripture quotations are from the New Revised Standard Version of the Bible, copyright © 1989, Division of Christian Education of the National Council of the Churches of Christ in the United States of America, and are used by permission.

Scripture quotations marked KJV are from the King James Version of the Bible.

Cover design by Tobias Becker, Bird Box Design.

Library of Congress Cataloging-in-Publication Data

Smith, Daniel P., 1938–
    Pathway to renewal : practical steps for congregations /
    Daniel P. Smith and Mary K. Sellon.
    p. cm.
ISBN 978-1-56699-371-5
1. Church management. 2. Church renewal.
    I. Sellon, Mary K. II. Title.

BV652.S57 2008
253—dc22
                    2008036041

        09 10 11 12   VP   5 4 3 2

TABLE OF CONTENTS

FOREWORD BY ALICE MANN   vii

PREFACE   xi

PROLOGUE
The Carpenter and the Unbuilder   1

CHAPTER 1
Congregational Renewal: What It Is and
What It Requires   5

CHAPTER 2
The Big Challenges of Congregational Renewal   31

CHAPTER 3—PHASE 1 OF RENEWAL
Developing Readiness: Preparing the Leaders to Lead   53

CHAPTER 4—PHASE 2 OF RENEWAL
Surfacing a Guiding Vision: Expanding the
Congregation's Openness to God   79

CHAPTER 5—PHASE 3 OF RENEWAL
Living into the Vision: Aligning the Work of
the Congregation with the Vision   111

CHAPTER 6
A Primer on Planning   139

EPILOGUE
The Carpenter and the Unbuilder   159

APPENDIX A
Group Exercises for Personal Formation   163

APPENDIX B
Processes to Help Surface a Vision   169

APPENDIX C
Powerful Questions   177

RESOURCES FOR FURTHER EXPLORATION   181

FOREWORD

In 1969, just as I was graduating from college, I had my first experience of attending a big church meeting. It was the annual convention of an Episcopal diocese, where a key official reported that a large number of constituent congregations were "marginal parishes," likely to die within ten to twenty years. It was, to say the least, a sobering introduction to the subject of congregational development and church vitality.

For the next thirty-nine years—my whole adult life within the church—this same conversation has been in progress across many denominations, faith groups, and geographical regions. To be sure, the discussion has gone through a number of phases—debates about which statistics we should believe, which culprits we should blame, which vocabulary we should use, which styles of renewal we should embrace. But, through it all, a good many North American congregations—along with their denominational partners—have tried to take the conversation deeper, to wrestle with more profound questions:

- Why don't things seem to be working for us the way they did in the years after World War II? Why does trying harder make so little difference in the outcome?

- What is the fundamental purpose of a church (or a synagogue) within our religious tradition? What sources of authority and inspiration can we, as a congregation, draw upon as we seek to clarify our faith identity and religious purpose?

- What realities in our local community and wider culture must we address if we are going to fulfill our deepest purpose today? How about ten years from now?

- What congregational strengths are we called to build upon as we move forward? And what familiar patterns are we called to relinquish or change?

- And finally, how will we survive the "journey through the wilderness"—the long period of questioning, learning, and transformation that is inevitably required of congregations that travel a path of renewal, revitalization, or redevelopment?

In contrast to the situation in 1969, an enormous body of literature about congregational vitality and transformation is available to church leaders today. It is so big, in fact, that one might wonder whether there is anything left to say, any fresh insight one can offer. But when we are in honest conversation—with God, with each other, with the world around us—about a question that really matters, new voices and new perspectives constantly emerge to lead us forward.

Daniel Smith and Mary Sellon Huycke are not new voices in the field of congregational revitalization. Since launching their joint consulting practice five years ago, Mary and Dan have produced two helpful volumes: *Redeveloping the Congregation* and *Practicing Right Relationship*. But this creative team is now taking us beyond the usual limits of helpful concepts and good advice (important enough resources in themselves). In *Pathway to Renewal: Practical Steps for Congregations,* these two seasoned guides offer to serve as our "wilderness outfitters." For any church leader wise enough to seek their expert help, they provide in this book a briefing on the overall conditions we are about to face; a map and compass for continuous navigation; backpacks carefully filled with the right equipment and supplies; and instruction on how to recognize that mysterious pillar formation—cloud by day and fire by night—that will tell us when to pause, when to move forward, and which direction to go.

Pathway to Renewal carefully distinguishes three phases of the wilderness journey: first, building the readiness of leaders to lead; second, developing a vision; and finally, aligning the congregation's life with the vision it has discerned. In their descriptions of these phases, the authors integrate wisdom from many sources into a coherent stream of guidance. One distinctive and helpful feature of this work is the authors' emphasis on the *different* leadership teams required as a congregation moves through the phases:

- an ad hoc *germination group* to get the conversation going and generate a spark of new energy;

- a more formally constituted *renewal task force* to help the church board assess the need for renewal and define some initial steps;

- a *vision team* to widen the circle of discussion and take the congregation into deeper discernment of God's particular call at this time in their history; and finally,

- a *balcony team* to support the board and the ministry leaders as they put the vision into practice by keeping track of the big picture, noticing when additional planning or adjustment is needed, and reminding the congregation of the commitments it has made.

In *Pathway to Renewal*, the role and task of each of these groups is carefully described and clues are offered to help the congregation determine when it is time to transition from one type of renewal leadership to the next. In each phase, the roles of pastor and board are identified and honored. I believe that this particular aspect of the book will become a reference point for future theory and practice in congregational transformation.

One final word to the reader: Wilderness outfitters don't come cheap, and any would-be adventurer has to make the full investment—not only purchasing their services (buying or borrowing the book) but also investing enough *time* to learn the lore thoroughly, enough *energy* to complete the physical preparation, and enough *humility* to revisit the field manual at each new turn of the road. There is no avoiding mistakes or surprises in this kind of journey—but we can, at least, ponder the experience of those who've been this way before whenever we are facing a weighty decision.

I wish you a splendid adventure. I don't know exactly how things will turn out for your specific church. But just as in the ancient spiritual discipline of walking the labyrinth, if your heart keeps trusting God and your feet keep taking the next forward step, you are guaranteed to find your way home.

ALICE MANN
Senior Consultant
The Alban Institute

PREFACE

"Going to church" has been an important element in both of our lives for most of our lifetimes. That being said, the little phrase "going to church" has acquired a very different meaning for us across the years.

When we were young, it meant putting on nice clothes and walking into a building at a prescribed time on either Sunday morning or Wednesday evening.

Across the years, a myriad of people and congregations have helped us attach a different meaning to that phrase. They have taught us that church isn't a building but a group of people who are committed to understanding and practicing the teachings of Christ. Church, then, is the web of relationships formed by these people, and it's the container in which they practice with each other how to love and serve and forgive. The idea is that if you can learn to see and respond to the God in nice Mrs. Valquez sitting in the pew in front of you and sometimes-cranky Mr. Holmes, who sits behind, then it's a bit easier to be Christlike to the scary teenager on the bus to work.

"Going to church" has, for us, come to mean a moment of stepping into a community where people are present to one another and to God, provoking insight and growth—community that calls out the best in each person, as people encourage one another to discover their gifts and to challenge each other to use them in service of goals that matter to the person and to God. Such moments have changed us. We hunger for more, and we are not alone.

We live in a time of spiritual yearning. People are hungry for this kind of transformative community and are seeking it in all kinds of settings other than organized religion and the Christian church. That saddens us, because we know that something miraculous and transformational happens when, in a caring community, those yearnings and the gospel are connected for a person. Not only is the experience life-giving for the individual; but then he or she also becomes God's life-giving agent in the world. We have seen individuals experience new levels of hope, deepen their capacity for compassion, and move beyond seemingly impossible limitations to help others create a new and more life-giving future. We have seen congregations create restorative relationships in fractured communities and bring God's loving and renewing presence into the world in concrete ways.

At the same time, a great many people in congregations still understand "going to church" as putting on nice clothes and walking into a building at a prescribed time on Sunday morning. People commonly tell us that they come home from church thinking it was "nice," but wanting it to be more than just nice. Our heart goes out to those people and congregations. As we sit with them, we hear their longing for "something more" and their uncertainty about what to do to make things different. Often, we hear their despair. These hard but honest conversations are the seeds of a new future—a new way of being church.

This book would not be possible without what we have learned from other people. We're grateful to the many consultants and researchers who share through both conversation and publications their experience and learning about how people, groups, congregations, and organizations change. Even more important for us have been our experiences with congregations and clergy as they have sensed God nudging them to find the pathway to renewal. As consultants and coaches for numerous congregations, pastors, and judicatory leaders, we have learned, with them, what works and what doesn't. As we have led workshops across the United States and Canada, participants have led us to new "aha's" and have refined our understandings.

What we offer are not merely theories. We have walked with and observed congregations, laity, and clergy as they have lived the steps and used the processes we describe. We know that congregational renewal is possible.

Blessings on you as you follow God's call to you and your congregation. May it lead you to the church you and God have always dreamed of.

PROLOGUE

The Carpenter and the Unbuilder

The Invitation

Once upon a time there was a man living in a certain kingdom who received an invitation from his king to come to dinner. Something inside him was excited as never before by the invitation. Something was afraid as well. Would he have the right clothes to wear? Would his manners be good enough for his lord's table? What would they talk about when they were not eating? Above all, the man was frightened by the long journey to the king's castle.

So what did the man do? Well, he spent one month deciding what to wear and buying the clothes he did not already have. He spent two months learning the rules of etiquette and practicing them as he ate. He spent three months reading up on all the latest issues faced by the kingdom so he would have something to say.

Finally he faced the journey itself. By trade the man was a carpenter. He built small houses and extra outhouses and garages better than anyone else. After he had packed the clothing and food he thought he would need for the journey, he had room for only a little more. So he decided to pack a few tools, enough to permit him to build adequate overnight shelter on the journey. Then he started out.

The first day he traveled through the morning and early afternoon, stopping only to eat some lunch. Then he set about constructing a rough shelter to spend the night in. After a few hours of labor he had a small, safe, dry place to sleep. The next morning as he was about to start out again, he looked at the shelter he had built. He began to notice places where it could be improved. So instead of resuming the journey right away, he began to make improvements on his little dwelling. Well, one thing led to another, garage to kitchen to indoor plumbing, and so on. Soon, he had pretty much forgotten about the invitation and the journey.

Meanwhile the king was beginning to wonder about the man. And so, as kings are able to do, he arranged for another person who was also traveling to the dinner to stop by and see how the man was coming along.

When the king's friend found him, the carpenter was living in his second house. He had sold the first one to someone, remembered the invitation, and moved on for a day or so. However, he had soon settled in and built an even bigger and better house on the profits he had made from the sale of his first one. The carpenter was only too happy to invite the visitor in for lunch; but while he was content to accept the offer of food, the visitor said he preferred to eat out in the yard under a tree.

"Is there a reason you don't want to come inside?" asked the carpenter, immediately wondering if his house wasn't quite right in some way.

"Why yes," replied the visitor. "You see, I am on a journey to have dinner with the king of our land. It is important for me to stay on the journey. Perhaps after lunch you would like to come with me?"

"What you say sounds familiar to me," said the carpenter. "I think I too received an invitation to have dinner with the king, but I have been a little bit uncertain of the way."

"I know," responded the stranger. "I was once uncertain as well. As a matter of fact, once I was a carpenter just like you. I too wanted to build safe places along the way to stay in. One day, another person on the journey helped me learn how to unbuild instead of to build. He helped me leave the house I was living in and trust the journey itself. I was worried about following the right path. He told me that there were a number of paths that would lead to the dinner. The king had set it up that way, and the king had also set up warnings along the wrong paths. The important thing was simply to put one foot in front of the other with love and trust. I was also worried about what I had left behind. To this he said that the king had seen to it that everything worth saving would be at the castle waiting for me."

"What you say is certainly of comfort. It helps to know that you have been just like me," said the carpenter.

"Well then, why don't we let go of this house and get on with the journey?"

"I don't know. Maybe. Can I sleep on it?"

"I suppose."

"May I fix a bed for you?"

"No," countered the visitor. "I will just stay out here under the tree. It is easier to notice the wonderful things the king has put along the way when you aren't looking out from inside something you have put up to protect yourself."

The unbuilder waited outside all night. The next morning the carpenter indeed had decided to resume the journey. Together they prepared to set out.

"Well," asked the carpenter. "Which way shall we go?"

"Which way seems right to you?" replied the unbuilder.

"I'm not sure."

"I'll tell you what. Let's just sit here a few minutes and think hard about the king. Remember the stories you have been told about him. Remember how much you love him. Remember how much he loves you. When you have remembered as clearly as you think you can, consider the paths that lie before you and see which one seems to satisfy your longing for, and remembrance of, the king. Let your desire to be with the king become more powerful in you than your uncertainty and fear about choosing the right or wrong path."

Silently they sat through the morning in the carpenter's front yard. Slowly it began to seem as though they were already on the journey. As that feeling grew and grew, it suddenly didn't seem like any decision needed to be made; it just happened. With a deep sense of freedom they were off.

Many of the days went just like that, new steps out of silent beginnings and pure desires. They simply waited until the sense of journeying wrapped itself around even their waiting, and then they were off without worrying whether they were on the "right" path or not. In the stillness of their hearts they made room for the path and the path seemed to come to them.

Of course the carpenter still felt the need to build a home from time to time. The unbuilder made sure he understood what he was doing and then let him do it if he really wanted to. While the carpenter labored, the unbuilder, his guide and friend, would continue the silent waiting in the yard under a tree, and soon they would unbuild yet another house and begin the journey again.

In the meantime the king kept the food warm, which he was very good at doing.

[The story is concluded in the epilogue.]

1
Congregational Renewal
WHAT IT IS AND WHAT IT REQUIRES

The church is not a building, the church is not a steeple,
the church is not a resting place, the church is a people.
I am the church. You are the church. . . .
Yes, we're the church together. *

"Finances are tight, and our numbers are dwindling. The congregation is looking to me to turn things around. So is my denomination—that's exactly what I was told when I was appointed here. And, frankly, that's my expectation too. Isn't that my job?" Janna, pastor of a United Methodist congregation that has been experiencing decline for many years, voices the belief of many congregations, denominations, and pastors: when a congregation is declining, it is the pastor's job to fix it.

Here's the hard truth. If you're a layperson in a congregation that's experiencing decline, whether the congregation thrives is ultimately up to you and the other members. Your pastor can teach, guide, lead, support, inspire, even cajole. But in the end, congregational health is a function of how people in the congregation relate to one another, to God, and to their community. A congregation is a microcosm of the greater church, a local embodiment of the body of Christ. In John's Gospel, Jesus says, "I came that they may have life, and have it abundantly" (John 10:10). We believe this is

When a congregation is truly being church, people:
- find hope,
- experience belonging,
- extend and receive forgiveness, and
- discover a sense of purpose and direction.

one of the primary messages that a healthy congregation embodies for its members and its surrounding community.

A congregation that is truly being church brings people into a loving, life-giving relationship with God and others that is transformational. This is the nature of the kin-dom of God, where covenant relationships model the best aspects of family. People find hope. They experience belonging; they extend and receive forgiveness. They discover a sense of purpose and direction. They learn to live with appreciation and joy no matter what the circumstances. Although a pastor can preach and teach this message, the message has power only to the extent that the people in the congregation live it and practice it with one another. Practicing loving, life-giving relationships transforms congregation members. Witnessing such benefits draws others who want something similar for themselves and their families.

Businesses are based on the premise of offering something of value—goods or services—to a customer in exchange for money. Successful businesses "give value for money." Gimmicks and fancy features may bring people through the door, but people won't buy unless they believe they'll receive something of worth. And they'll return and recommend the business to others only if they receive something of value. Congregations are not businesses, yet they can fall into a similar trap of thinking that it's the features and the gimmicks that people want. A congregation's greatest asset, the unique gift it offers, is the people who make up the congregation and the possibilities for transformation they embody.

When we talk about congregational renewal, we mean a renewal of the people's ability to notice and experience God in their midst, a renewal of the congregation's desire to partner with God in achieving God's aims for the world. The term renewal implies that the congregation knew how to do this at one time and that the work is a reclaiming of a lost skill. We find that's not always the case. Some congregations we've worked with have no memory of ever having been a church that talked openly about God and matters of faith. The people have no memory of the congregation's ever having had an evangelistic bent. However, we have yet to encounter a congregation that, when asked to recall moments when its church was really "being church," couldn't name sacred moments when God seemed present and people found healing and hope.

The church-growth movement is often blamed for leading congregations down the path of thinking that bigger is better and that increased numbers equal health and growth. That movement did, however, help raise the question of how to measure congregational health. If the measure is not dollars in the bank or people in the pews, what is it? We hear congregations and pastors wrestling with questions that weren't on the table twenty years ago. "What's the fundamental purpose of church? What difference is a congregation supposed to make in the lives of its members and in its surrounding community? What does it mean to be a follower of Jesus? What does it mean to be spiritual? What difference do spiritual practices make?"

When we hear people wrestling with questions like these, we smile. These challenging questions are the foundation of renewal, the building blocks of a new future. They are not, however, the point at which most congregations start. Fear of having to close the church or to reduce the services offered to members typically prompts a congregation's desire for renewal: "We need to do something now, if we're going to still be open a decade from now." This desire to avoid death drives many renewal efforts, and it certainly provides energy. But if the congregation

What's renewed in congregational renewal is the people's understanding of their relationship with God, their relationship with their community, and their sense of calling.

itself doesn't ultimately trade its fear of death for a longing for life, the efforts will end as soon as the danger has passed.

The aim of renewal is not a bigger building or high-tech worship or a slew of professional programs, but a new way of looking at church, the work of a congregation, and what it has to offer the world. Congregational renewal is a renewal of the people's understanding of their relationship with God, their relationship with their community, and their calling. In the most fundamental sense, congregational renewal happens through "people renewal."

No pastor, no program, no resource can make renewal happen. On the other hand, almost any pastor, program, or resource can help renewal unfold when the people of a congregation deeply desire a new and better life and are willing to do what it takes to get there. The hard part can be developing that desire. As long as life together is satisfactory, there is little impetus for change.

Often congregations first start talking about renewal because demographic changes in the community are affecting them. On a barrier island of New Jersey, wealthy summer residents now dominate the once primarily working-class community. The long-standing community church wonders how long it can stay open. In a small town in California, 75 percent of those now living in the neighborhood around the Presbyterian church speak primarily Spanish. In a neighborhood of Seattle, the new neighbors of the United Methodist church are young families stretched for time and money who have little or no church background. In each case, the declining local church provides an accurate historical snapshot of the people who lived in the neighborhood thirty years ago and what they valued.

Over and over we hear congregations wishing that the people in the community would become active in their church. What drives that desire is revealed in their response to the question "Why?" Any time a significant number of people answer, "To keep our programs running and our doors open," we know that the congregation is in trouble. It has moved to the point at which the people beyond its doors are valued primarily for what they can bring to the church. People in the community are seen as the congregation's salvation, rather than the other way around.

Attempting to lure the new population group, the congregational leaders add programs and make changes they imagine will appeal to the people. Surprised and frustrated when their changes show little result, they redouble their efforts to find the right program. This work is misdirected. The congregation is not declining because the community around it has changed, or even primarily because the church's form of ministry and worship feels foreign to those in the neighborhood. The real and deeper issue is that the congregation has lost connection with a Christian church's basic mission: helping people experience God and connect with the gospel message of life and hope.

Without this sense of mission to keep the congregation focused beyond the doors of the church, the congregation turns inward and loses connection with its community. Only when the congregation's well-being is threatened does the issue of connecting with its community arise. All of its efforts however, are infused with a mind-set and a heart-set that value strengthening and preserving the congregation over serving the needs of the people in the community with whom members and leaders

---

Declining congregations have lost connection with the Christian church's basic mission of helping people experience God and live the gospel message of life and hope.

---

want to connect. This approach never works. People know when they're being used. Before others will turn to a congregation as a life-giving resource in their lives, the congregation has to be a place that offers life. When traveling by plane, passengers are reminded that in the event of an emergency they should put on their own oxygen masks before helping others. In congregational renewal, a congregation reminds itself of and intentionally engages in the basic practices of Christianity. It realigns itself with the basic outward-focused mission of church.

Each denomination has its own way of describing this work. Each congregation has its own emphasis. We've heard it said that congregations lean toward either the great commandment—love God and love your neighbor as yourself (Matt. 22:34–40) —or the great commission: go forth and make disciples (Matt. 28:16–20). Although both are found in Matthew's Gospel, we find that people generally do emphasize one over the other. While able to engage in acts of love directed toward the neighbor, many pastors and congregations we talk with express a deep ambivalence about disciple-making. They wonder if evangelism has a place in today's world. At the same time, they tell us that they rarely talk about these doubts with anyone. This inner and unspoken conflict has left many congregations unsure of what their "good news" is and why they should share it, let alone how to share it. They don't know the value they offer.

What Happened to Our Church?

It's easy to blame the decline of a congregation on a series of "bad" pastors or a dramatic shift in the demographics of the community. And without a doubt, many portions of North America are less church-friendly than they were fifty years ago. Although these externals can certainly contribute to and exacerbate decline, they generally aren't the real reasons for it. A decline in congregational health has both an outer and an inner component. The outer, more visible aspect of decline is the weakening of the congregation as an organization. The less visible but more damaging facet of decline is the congregation's understanding of itself and its purpose. Let's look first, however, at the organizational aspect and what commonly happens to congregations across time.

Congregations are organizations, formal associations of people who come together for a common purpose. Organizations, much like living organisms, move through predictable stages of development. So common is this phenomenon that we think of it as a natural aging process. We identify the stages a congregation goes through as conception and birth, creative formation, performing stability, protective maintenance, and crisis and confusion.

The Aging Process of a Congregation

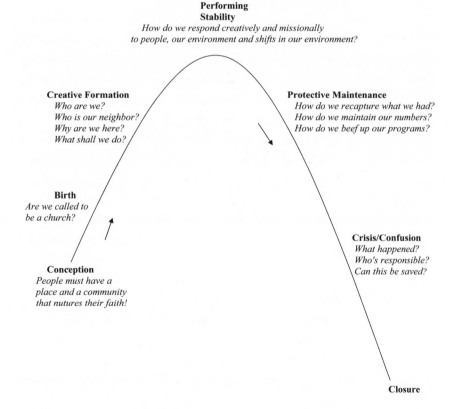

**Performing
Stability**
*How do we respond creatively and missionally
to people, our environment and shifts in our environment?*

Creative Formation
*Who are we?
Who is our neighbor?
Why are we here?
What shall we do?*

Protective Maintenance
*How do we recapture what we had?
How do we maintain our numbers?
How do we beef up our programs?*

Birth
*Are we called to
be a church?*

Crisis/Confusion
*What happened?
Who's responsible?
Can this be saved?*

Conception
*People must have a
place and a community
that nutures their faith!*

Closure

Conception and Birth

Ideally, congregations are conceived out of a missionary zeal and birthed by a small group of people who have experienced the foundational difference Christ makes in their lives. These people believe deeply that developing a relationship with God in the manner of Jesus can make a tremendous difference in people's lives and, through them, in the world. With this conviction, they set about creating a place and a community where other people can be introduced to and nurtured in Christian discipleship.

The birth of the Bothell United Methodist Church is typical. In 1885 Mary Ann and David Bothell looked out at their small town and saw people moving in. They had high hopes for the growth of their community and were pleased to see friendships and business relationships forming. Concerned that they saw no place for faith and spirituality to be nurtured, they concluded, "This is not acceptable."

Not knowing what to do, but convinced that something had to be done, they invited sixteen people to their home for hymn singing, Scripture reading, and sharing. This fellowship grew quickly, and soon twenty-five families in the village were gathering for regular times of worship, spiritual nurture, and the development of caring relationships. The group, in time, began asking, "Are we called to be a church and to bring what we've found to others?" They answered yes, even though they weren't fully sure what that call would entail. Their sense of being called by God for a specific purpose spurred them to move beyond what had become familiar and comfortable. The people did what was needed to connect with and meet the spiritual needs of others.

Creative Formation

A period of creative formation follows this ideal birth, as the people figure out who they are as a congregation and what shape their life together will take. As they talk and work together, they form answers to fundamental questions: "Who are we? Who is our neighbor? What does God want for this place and these people? What's our part in what God wants to accomplish?" And, once those questions are answered: "What shall we do and how shall we do it?" Their focus is outward, on the impact they want to have on the wider world. "What's the difference God wants for others and for this community? Let's roll up our sleeves and get busy!"

As the people create together, they experience energy and grow in faith, both as individuals and as a community. At this stage, everything is a "first"; no one says, "We've never done it like this before." It is an exciting and magnetic time. God's presence is felt; everything seems touched by God's Spirit. Drawn to the congregation's energy and joy, people come and join with the members and find their lives changed in positive ways. As the congregation develops, administrative and physical structures are created as needed to support and house the work. Roadblocks arise, but no challenge seems to block the people for long. The congregation's clear, deep commitment, combined with relationships that are mutual and generative, allows it to address creatively whatever comes along. The congregation at this stage in its life is best described as a movement—a growing network of people with a common passion working together to achieve a common aim.

Performing Stability

As the people of the congregation continue working together, patterns develop and norms are set. Life becomes more predictable, and the church moves into a period marked by both outward extension and inner stability. The congregation is firmly attached to achieving a common aim while enjoying stable institutional structures that advance its work. The congregation is successful both in introducing people to Christian discipleship and in supporting them in their ongoing development. Typically, at this stage in its life the congregation has sufficient human and financial resources to create a highly rewarding

A key factor in congregational decline is the failure to introduce new members to and equip them in the disciple-making mission of the church.

communal life in addition to supporting its primary work of making disciples. Its mission, its understanding of what it means to be church, guides the congregation's decision making and its life together. The congregation seems continually to be responding to an unspoken question: "How do we respond creatively and missionally to people, our environment, and shifts in our environment?"

The congregation, in this stage of its life, still maintains a distinctive outward focus. Leaders and members ask, "Whom does God want us to see and serve? How can we best nurture discipleship?" At the same time, the congregation finds more of its time and energy being taken up by administrative and building-related demands. Commitment to achieving a particular mission is paired with stable and functional organizational structures. At this point, the congregation is a movement housed in an institution.

Over time, the congregation experiences internal change. It just happens. Key leaders move away. Newcomers arrive with new passions, new gifts. Most significant, the majority of people drawn to the congregation stay because the church serves their needs. This motive is in marked contrast to what attracted the earliest church members—the opportunity to help create a place that served the spiritual needs of others. If the congregation does not introduce new members to and equip them in the disciple-making mission of the church, an increasing percentage of church members become consumers of the church's services rather than providers. The congregation's mission shifts from creating a place for others to maintaining a place for its own members. This shift is a key factor in congregational decline.

Protective Maintenance

If this loss of a missional heart is not detected and corrected, the culture of the church will start to shift—from a mode of missional zeal and high creativity to one of protective maintenance. Members feel protective toward the culture and the programs that proved effective in their own lives: "It worked fine for me and still does, so why change it?" Content with what they experience, the members focus on maintaining and improving what's already there.

The early stages of protective maintenance are easily missed. Energy seems just a bit off, getting folk to help out with the ministries a tad more difficult. Everyone has an explanation: "It was a snowy winter . . . a beautiful summer . . . people are just real busy right now." Attendance may drop a little, but that too gets explained away: "I don't think Jim is counting those folks who come in late." When the loss is finally addressed, the driving questions become "How do we recapture what we had? How do we maintain our numbers? How do we beef up our programs?"

People are truly proud of their church and take pleasure in sharing it with visitors. Church members like the difference that church involvement makes in their lives. In this stage of the congregation's life, however, the majority of members can't readily explain what that difference is. Instead, they point to features they appreciate. People share their "church" rather than their faith. "Come hear our preacher—she's great." "Come to the Christmas cantata; our choir is terrific."

At the same time the congregation is experiencing these changes, other changes are taking place in the community around the church. Local industries open and close. Demographics shift. New groups of people arrive, bringing with them their own cultural preferences and unique sets of gifts and needs. And beyond the immediate community, the world shifts.

When the congregation was at its best, it was aware of both the internal and the external changes taking place; it adapted in whatever ways were needed to live out its mission successfully. At the congregation's heart was a passionate commitment to make a particular difference. It looked for God in each moment and sought to align itself with God's aims. It lived in the present and walked with intention into the future. As a congregation moves more deeply into protective maintenance, it focuses increasingly on the past. The emphasis becomes protecting what God has already done and the previously successful forms of programming, leadership, and ways of relating through which the congregation experienced God.

Concerned with its own well-being, the congregation, often without realizing it, ignores or minimizes the importance of the changes taking place in the surrounding community and the wider world. The preservation of the church as institution becomes more important than its mission. When the mission dies, the congregation begins to die.

As this stage progresses, the signs of decline become more visible: worship attendance declines; financial stability slips; fewer visitors become members. Believing that any problem can be reversed, members put their efforts into working harder at what worked in the past. When that approach fails, a new program is added, a campaign mounted, or a change in pastors initiated.

Newcomers are valued for the way they enhance the experience of current members. One woman put it this way: "I'm always delighted to see newcomers in worship. Worship feels better to me when the seats are full." Another put it more bluntly: "We need new people so that the church can stay open." Events publicized to the community (like rummage sales and pancake breakfasts) are thinly disguised fund raisers designed to help the church meet its financial goals and obligations. The church becomes vampirelike, feeding off the energy and resources of its surrounding community.

The result is a self-absorbed, inward-focused congregation. In crass terms, it's as if the employees of McDonald's came to work each day and focused all their energy on feeding each other. They go home feeling successful; they know they've worked hard, that they've fed one another and fed themselves. A business can't get away with that for long, but a church can survive in that mode for as long as the money holds out.

Crisis and Confusion

Once the money runs low, the congregation generally grows more open to trying any strategy that promises to fix the church. When the fixes don't work, frustration rises, blaming increases, relationships deteriorate, and the slide escalates until finally the congregation arrives at the point of crisis and confusion. The foremost questions for the congregation become: "What happened? Who's responsible? Can this church be saved?"

The congregation finally faces an unavoidable decision: "Are we going to have to close our doors?" Some congregations, sensing that their work is done, choose to close while they still have some control over the process. Others, either unsure of what to do or afraid or unwilling to do what it takes, choose to do nothing. They continue on the path of decline until their resources are gone and they're forced to close. And some congregations, sensing that God still has work for them, give themselves up to the process of renewal.

Organizational renewal is ideally addressed while a congregation is still in the stage of performing stability. The sense of being a movement is still strong. Attachment to institutional forms is relatively low. Congregations tend not to reflect on issues of renewal at this point in their lives, however. Why spend time and energy fixing something that doesn't appear to be broken? Most congregations wait until the level of discomfort rises to the point at which it can no longer be ignored. By then, the congregation is faced with a major task: transforming a congealed institution into a fresh and impassioned movement.

Were organizational transformation the only aspect of change to be considered, renewal would still be a considerable challenge.

Take a look at the business section of your local bookstore or do a Web search for organizational renewal, and be prepared to find a flood of resources. Leading organizational change is extraordinarily challenging. That said, the challenge facing congregations that need to change is doubly so.

In a business and in the majority of nonprofit organizations, leaders determine the purpose, the product, and the norms that will govern behavior. In this era, leaders work hard to function collaboratively and to bring people along with them. But ultimately, their will is imposed on the rest of the organization. The employees of a shoe factory make the shoes that management decides will be made. As long as the workers work and the shoes get made and customers buy them, the factory does fine. Management may want employees to be dedicated to the purpose and values of the company and to get along well with each other. Positive attitudes enhance the efficiency of the operation. But in the end, the company's product can be produced regardless of employee attitudes.

That's not true for the church. While the people in the pews do the work, just as the employees of a company do, in a church the product finally is a community that embodies the mind and heart of Christ. A congregation may produce good works and show signs of organizational strength, but the unique transformational aims of church require the work to be done in a particular way with a particular attitude. Only with a Christlike mind-set and heart-set will a church embody the kin-dom of God and align itself in service to the well-being of the world.

A congregation can produce good works and show signs of organizational strength and still be in decline.

Marks of Health and Indicators of Decline

Congregational decline is, at heart, an inner matter. It's a reflection of a congregation's abandoning its fundamental purpose of embodying church, being a community that brings people into a loving, life-giving, transformational relationship with God, with one another, and with the world. When we assess a congregation's vitality, we look for three marks of inner health:

- continual spiritual formation as an essential for everyone rather than an activity pursued by some

- relationships among people that embody the kin-dom of God; relationships that are honoring, forgiving, loving, caring, mutual, and generative

- a deep, pervasive concern for the temporal and spiritual well-being of those beyond the doors of the church—a concern that manifests in action

These are indicators that the congregation is an embodiment of the biblical concept of church as modeled by the early church in New Testament writings. They provide a way to look inside the heart and mind of a congregation. Yet a congregation may appear to be outwardly healthy according to its organizational stage of life—for example, to be in the creative formation stage, and still not be inwardly so; that is, and not embody church. Mainline denominations are investing huge amounts of time, energy, and money in trying to start new congregations. It is important for them to find ways to ensure that these hallmarks of congregational health are present from the start. Starting intentionally healthy Christlike congregations can be challenging when the laity and clergy working to start these congregations have limited or no experience in being part of such a faith community.

When assessing inner health, we look also for five indicators of decline. These tendencies cripple a congregation. When they are present in the early stages of a congregation's life, that congregation doesn't grow to become much more than a service club. Service clubs are fine organizations, but congregations are called to be something else. These tendencies can also develop later in a congregation's life. When this is the case, these shifts in how the congregation functions and views its purpose drive the transition from performing stability to protective maintenance. By the time the shifts are evident, the congregation has come to see this way of being and doing church as normal. At this point, a new inward-focused trajectory has been set. For this reason, we consider any church that exhibits these tendencies a declining congregation. Decline may not yet be detectable in the statistics the church uses to measure success, but it's simply a matter of time.

How do we define decline? A declining congregation gives itself to:

- growing the church rather than witnessing to faith
- running the church rather than forming disciples
- being people-led rather than being Spirit-led
- participating in mission projects without having a mission
- fixing rather than creating

Growing the church, running the church, being people-led, participating in mission projects, and fixing can all, at certain times, serve a congregation and contribute to health. However, when these become the primary focus, the congregation is in serious trouble. Congregational renewal efforts must address these foundational issues of health rather than simply developing and strengthening the institution. We value a developed and strong institution—but that strength needs to be a fruit of a faithful congregation, not its primary aim. And a fruitful congregation develops only through the continual spiritual formation of the congregation's members.

In a declining congregation, members share their church rather than their faith.

To help you assess whether your congregation is in need of renewal, let's take a closer look at these five hallmarks of declining congregations:

People Focus on Growing the Church Rather than on Witnessing to Faith

Conversations focus on the nuts and bolts of running the church or the events and concerns of daily life. Members are out of touch with their own faith stories and how their lives have been changed through their own spiritual formation. They don't know how to talk with others about God and faith issues. Members share their church, rather than their faith, with people.

A declining congregation views people outside its doors more in terms of what they can bring to the church than in terms of the life-changing difference the church can make for them. Visitors who look as though they would fit in and have something to offer are warmly welcomed. Those who seem out of the ordinary or needy may be noticed, but they receive very different treatment. The marginalized and hurting people in the community are viewed not as potential pew-mates or fellow disciples, but as recipients of the church's benevolence.

Efforts Focus on Running the Church Rather than on Forming Disciples

The congregation sees its work as offering classes, activities, and services rather than nurturing the spiritual and faith development of people. It is attached to offering certain programs and ministries and to carrying them out in particular ways. Tiring, yet needing to have these activities staffed, the congregation sees newcomers as resources to be mined. Faithfulness is defined by a person's willingness to do what's needed to keep the church running.

In a declining congregation, efforts serve the preservation of the institution. People attend meetings because they're on the calendar. What the church needs to keep it running takes precedence over what the participants need to grow as disciples of Christ. Leaders spend time and energy enticing and motivating people to serve on committees and to take on tasks, rather than creating opportunities and venues for their development as followers of Christ.

The Congregation Is People-led Rather than Spirit-led

People are confident in their ability to run the church and do not think of turning to God for guidance in running the church. Leaders strive to direct the church as a business, adopting the best practices of the business world, without undergirding those practices with a radical dependence on God.

The declining congregation depends on the pastor, church members, or other human experts for guidance and direction. Meetings are for business. They may include a token reading of Scripture or an opening prayer, but rarely if ever does a group think of bringing faith into the discussion at hand. People think of and refer to the church as "our church," not as "God's church."

The Congregation Engages in Mission Projects but Doesn't Have a Mission

There is likely a missions committee that plans several mission projects across a year's time. These projects flow out of and reinforce the congregation's self-image of being "mission-minded." Projects generally reflect not a shared missional aim of the congregation, but the mission interests of individuals or groups. Success is measured by the amount of support generated for the project and the degree of satisfaction the congregation derives from the work.

The declining congregation may have a mission statement printed at the top of the worship bulletin or posted on the narthex wall. That mission statement, however, is not used to align human and financial resources. Leaders may be able to recite it, but it does not drive planning. There's no shared and compelling sense of purpose underlying congregational life and ministry.

Leaders Focus on Fixing Rather than Creating

The member's strongest desire is to feel comfortable in the church. When challenges or new situations arise, people view them as problems to be solved so that the church can get back to normal, rather than as opportunities to move in a new direction. They feel most comfortable replicating what's been done before. Though this way of doing things saves a great deal of time and effort, it lacks the energy that comes from creating something new.

In a declining church, leaders strive to keep the congregation happy rather than to lead members in faithful living. Leaders are wary of taking risks and making mistakes. When faced with new challenges, congregational leaders look to others for their answers. They seek out experts—a new pastor, a consultant, denominational staff people, and the like—who will tell them what to do. At the same time, leaders and members balk at engaging in activities that seem new or different.

The Shifts Become the Norm

These inner shifts happen so gradually across the years that even the once-healthy congregation is unaware that changes have taken place. Members have no memory of those moments when decisions began to define a new way of being and "doing church." This shift of focus and attitude has been prevalent for so long in mainstream Protestant congregations that many people who have grown up in the church have never experienced anything else. Typically, so long as the church can maintain a satisfactory level of programming and services for the congregation, no one notices that anything is wrong.

Renewal is not just for "sick" congregations. Any congregation whose life together and decision making reveal a preference for serving itself rather than others, running a church rather than forming disciples, turning to the pastor or other leaders rather than to God, or supporting missions rather than having a mission, is at risk of decline. Destructive attitudes and values are already infiltrating the decision-making process. Just as with organizational renewal, the ideal time to address this renewal of heart and mind is at a time when everything is going well. If it is done then, before any shifts have become ingrained, the renewal is a matter of slight realignments. But most congregations don't address renewal then. "Things are fine. Why give energy to something that isn't causing us any problems?"

Once decline becomes noticeable, a significant shift in focus and attitudes has already taken root. But generally, congregations ignore the signs. Most congregations don't think about renewal until life has reached, or is nearing, a state of crisis and confusion. When a congregation finally does respond, it does so by moving into a "fix-it" mode. Seminars and books offer a myriad of solutions to a congregation's stall or decline—recommending that the congregation learn to welcome visitors more effectively, move to a growing suburb, renovate the nursery, upgrade marketing, add video screens to the worship space, change the music and the preaching style, or start a small-group ministry. When such "fixes" prove ineffective, the congregation then turns to the personnel committee, demanding that its members figure out what's wrong with the pastor and "fix" him or her. A new pastor may provide a shot of energy and hope, but most typically the congregation returns to its previous state in short order—if not during the tenure of that pastor, then after his or her departure.

The Work of Renewal

The church seeking renewal must look beyond simply improving its programs and its building, though both may ultimately be changed. Pastors and laity leading renewal in their declining congregations are asking people to make fundamental shifts in their perspectives, their attitudes, and their behaviors. The work demands a great deal from a people and a pastor. If you've ever remodeled a house while attempting to live in it, you have a sense of the chaos and complexity of congregational renewal. It will take far longer, cost you more, and prove messier than you ever imagined at the start. People who have worked with both church starts and church renewal will tell you that starting a church is "easy," compared to renewing one. The difficulty lies in the work itself. Pogo's line holds true: "We have met the enemy and he is us."

Your congregation is what it is today not because of what a bad pastor did to it, or because the neighborhood has changed, or because our culture is going to hell in a handbasket. Although those occurrences and many others have had an impact, your congregation is what it is today because of how it responded, or failed to respond, to the realities it faced. What your congregation will be in the future is up to you and the other members and how you work together to create something new from the realities you face.

What you do or don't do now will make the difference. Your actions will either reinforce the patterns that have become established in your congregation, or start to counter and shift them. The leadership provided by your pastor can help or hinder, but it cannot make your congregation succeed or keep it from ultimately achieving the goals you set for yourselves.

Renewal requires people to make fundamental shifts in their perspectives, their attitudes, and their behaviors.

The three phases of renewal:
- developing readiness
- surfacing a guiding vision
- living into the vision

Some wonder, "Is it even possible? Can people with little or no experience of their congregation's being church in this way create this kind of community?" We've seen it happen enough times to know that the hope is true and that renewal is possible—not easy, but possible. The path to renewal looks different for each congregation, but some common elements can be observed. Here's what we know.

Just as decline has outer and inner aspects, so does renewal. To move to a new place, a congregation must tend to both. Organizationally, there are three phases of work:

1. Developing readiness: preparing the leaders to lead the congregation in a new direction.
2. Surfacing a compelling congregational vision that will guide decision making.
3. Developing and implementing strategies that move the congregation toward the envisioned future.

These three fundamental tasks frame the work that ultimately realigns a congregation. Addressed sequentially, they break renewal up into understandable and manageable phases of work. The work of the first two phases culminates in pivotal decisions that prepare the congregation to tackle the final phase of work. Phase 1 results in leaders' declaring the congregation's current trajectory unacceptable and committing to lead in a new direction. Phase 2 results in a vision of a better future, discerned by the congregation and formally adopted by the congregation's leaders.

While making such decisions might be a simple thing for an individual, it takes a fairly long time for a congregation to make informed and "owned" choices. Whatever the congregation decides must be desired, claimed, and lived into. It's one thing to say that you want something; it's another to want it enough that you follow through and act on the intention. Phase 3 focuses on exactly that—creating the future that's been envisioned.

**The Organizational
Phases of Renewal**

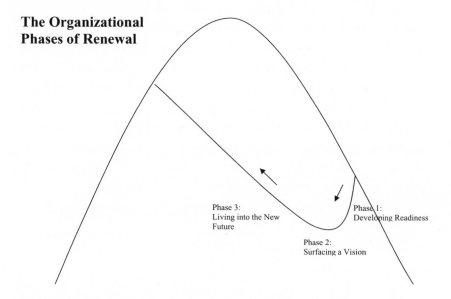

Phase 3:
Living into the New
Future

Phase 1:
Developing Readiness

Phase 2:
Surfacing a Vision

Each of these three phases demands significant work on the part of the people involved. The real work of renewal, however, is inner work. It is here that the greatest challenge lies. To complete these organizational tasks, the people of the congregation must make inner shifts, making the transition from one way of thinking about the congregation to quite another. During

---

The real work of renewal is inner work, making the transition from one way of thinking about the congregation to quite another.

---

renewal, people let go of what feels right and normal to create a new normal for themselves.

The congregation's inner work of transition has multiple steps. It begins with the recognition that something is wrong— that congregational life, while adequate, is missing something. Because a congregation is an outpost of the Christian church, the next step is to become anchored in a biblical and historical understanding of the purpose of church. When that purpose seems clear, the next step is to name and let go of preconceived notions about the form ministry should take. This step leads to a period of genuinely not knowing what to do. Rather than jumping in and filling that void with a quick solution, the challenge is to open ourselves to God and wait. From that place of expectant waiting, God's leading is sensed and a path forward is chosen. Finally, actions are aligned with intent, and a new way of being and doing church is created. The congregation moves through these steps of transition only as individuals in the congregation are able to move through these shifts.

The Inner Work of Renewal

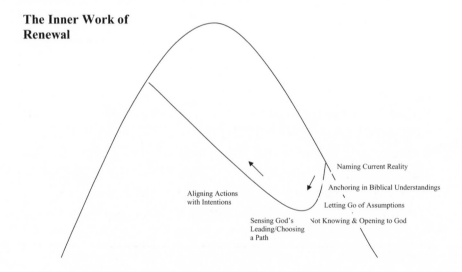

Naming Current Reality

Anchoring in Biblical Understandings

Aligning Actions with Intentions

Letting Go of Assumptions

Sensing God's Leading/Choosing a Path

Not Knowing & Opening to God

This inner work is the real work of renewal, and it is a work of the people. Pastors and outside consultants have much to offer, but they can't do the work for the people. Think of renewal as physical therapy for the body of Christ. The body is renewed as the people engage in practices that develop and strengthen the muscles of Christian discipleship and community. The chapters that follow describe in detail the work that needs to be done during each of the three main phases of renewal. They also provide insight and helpful ideas for how to help the people make the inner shifts each stage demands.

Taking Time to Reflect

We've given you a lot to think about. Take some time now to reflect on what you've just read. We hope that you're reading this book along with at least one other person from your congregation. Make time to get together with that person to have a conversation centered on the following questions. Go beyond simply reporting your answers. Give yourselves permission to probe beyond the initial words so that you understand each other's thoughts and feelings.

1. What excited you about this chapter? What challenged you? What "aha's" did you have? With whom would you most like to talk about the ideas in this chapter?

2. Think back on the various churches you've been a part of. Where in their life cycle do you think they stood? Where do you place your current church in its life cycle? Why?

3. The authors name three indicators of congregational health. On a scale of one to ten, with one being low and ten being high, score your congregation on each.

4. The authors name five hallmarks of declining congregations. On a scale of one to ten, with one being "doesn't

exhibit this at all" and ten being "this describes us exactly," where would you place your congregation in relation to each hallmark?

5. Today, on a scale of one to ten, with one being "not at all" and ten being "with all my heart," how much do you want the kind of renewal outlined by the authors? What contributes to your answer?

6. Today, on a scale of one to ten, with one being "not at all" and ten being "let's get going right now!" how willing are you to be a part of making sure that outcome happens? What would you need for your level of willingness to increase?

2

The Big Challenges of Congregational Renewal

Before turning to the details of each phase of renewal, we want to discuss some challenges you're likely to encounter, whether your congregation is large or small, urban or rural. These challenges make our list because of their capacity to frustrate people and stall the process. Even when the work is going well, renewal can seem messy and slow. When difficulties arise, people commonly conclude that they've done something wrong or that renewal is impossible. Most often, it's simply that the congregation has come head to head with one of renewal's big but natural challenges. When we teach on this topic or work with a congregation in the process of renewal, laypeople and clergy often express a sense of relief upon learning that their experiences are normal, not insurmountable roadblocks.

When the process of leading change in your congregation is driving you crazy, come back to this list. Use it to help you sort out what about the process is frustrating you or hindering movement forward. Part of your role as a leader will be to help the congregation maintain its focus and to continue to learn and grow when frustrations and challenges arise. Though few would call these moments enjoyable, they can be transformative for the congregation that works through them together. On the other side lie deepened relationships, expanded competence, and increased trust in God.

Changing the Culture of a Congregation Takes a Long Time

It took many years for your congregation to develop its current culture. By *culture* we mean your congregation's norms, the way of living and thinking that the congregation accepts as normal. These values and the established patterns of behavior that arise from them are so ingrained that no one even thinks about them. These cultural norms are just accepted as the "right" way to do things. Think about how your congregation shares information, selects leaders, and deals with conflict. If you find yourself saying, "Doesn't everybody do it that way?" or "Everybody *should* do it that way!" you have expressed a cultural norm. A group's norms provide stability and predictability; they ensure that what the group experiences tomorrow will be similar to what it experienced today. The culture of a declining congregation reinforces decline, and so the culture itself is what has to be renewed.

Cultural norms are patterns that feel normal and right, so substituting one set for another is a major endeavor. It will take years for your congregation's culture to change and for the new culture to seem normal to people. How many years? The truest answer we can give you is "as many years as it takes." We've never seen a congregation shift its culture in a lasting way in less than seven years. A good indicator that new norms have been set is that the shifts remain in place following a pastoral change. Often when a pastor leaves, a congregation that made significant shifts in how people live and work together reverts to its old norms. The fact that people agreed to make changes doesn't mean they've integrated those changes. If people don't find the new way of acting and interacting preferable, if they don't come to think of it as the

---

A group's norms provide stability and predictability.
The norms of a declining congregation reinforce decline.

Shifting the attitudes, preferences, and patterns of a congregation is slow work. It's normal for people to wonder whether their efforts are making a difference.

normal and "right" way, then as soon as the external pressure to comply disappears, so will the changes.

Some wonder why congregational renewal takes so long, since individuals can change their mind and life trajectory very quickly. When presented with an alternative path, a motorcycle can respond far more quickly than an eighteen-wheeler. Paul on the road to Damascus experienced a flash of blinding insight, and everything changed in an instant, whereas the Hebrew people took forty years to make their way to the promised land. An individual can make adjustments in her life much more readily than a group with its collection of many lives. Congregations function like any large group. The worldview of not just one person but many people must shift. Groups with a long history together, like most congregations, find change particularly slow and difficult. Patterns and traditions are set. When individuals push the boundaries, others in the group are quick to nudge them back.

Because shifting the attitudes, preferences, and patterns of a congregation is such slow work, it's normal for people to wonder whether their efforts toward change are making any difference. This uncertainty is particularly common in congregations that have attempted renewal or change efforts in the past and have failed. Such congregations are even more likely to give up when they don't see quick results. Faced with a monumental journey, leaders need to think in terms of small steps. What is the next baby step we need to take that would move us closer to our goal? How will we know when we've accomplished that? How does taking this step serve our long-term aim?

Watch for and celebrate moments that are a foretaste of the future you're working to create. These are signs of progress.

Because the journey is long, fresh planning must be done at each step of the way. No plan built today will serve five years from now. Frequent planning efforts and a regular revisiting of that planning serves the process, allowing the incorporation of new developments and fresh insights. Planning done this way is responsive and organic. It encourages regular assessment and adjustment. It provides a natural opportunity to reflect on and help others see the very real progress being made.

It's also important to detect and celebrate the events and interactions along the way which indicate that change is taking place. These short-term victories may be very different from what your congregation is used to getting excited about or even noticing. A congregation wanting improved relationships, but accustomed only to measuring the number of people attending worship services and the amount of money given, may not detect that conversations between members are becoming deeper. Watch for moments that are foretastes of the future you're working to create. These are signs that the congregation is making progress. If you're not used to looking for them, they're easy to miss.

Leaders need to help people learn to notice and recognize the meaning of these events that might otherwise be overlooked. As members learn to recognize signs of progress, their appreciation of and desire for the new culture often grow. These signs indicate that advances are being made in shifting the culture. Noticing these changes encourages people to keep at their efforts, to say, "Our work really *is* making a difference."

People Move at Their Own Pace

Frank and Janet serve on the governing board of their congregation. Last year they attended a workshop on renewal and came home convinced of their congregation's need for renewal and excited about the challenge. Talking to them six months later, however, we heard this: "We've run into an absolute stone wall," Frank confided. "We bring renewal up in meetings, but people ignore us and simply continue doing things the way they always have. I'm so frustrated that I'm thinking I should leave and find another church—one that gets it."

Present a group of people with a new idea or an innovation, and the response is predictable. A few individuals will adopt an innovative idea right off the bat. A few others will fall at the other end of spectrum and vehemently oppose it. In the middle will be everyone else, waiting to see what others think before they make their own decision.

The work of sociologist and statistician Everett Rogers helps us understand this phenomenon. Rogers's Diffusion Theory proposes that when a new idea or innovation is presented to a social system, the people in the system adopt that idea or innovation at different rates. Innovators, 2.5 percent of the group, make their decision rapidly and independently. If the idea captivates them and makes sense to them, they're in. The remaining 97.5 percent look to the choices others in the group are making to help them decide.

Innovation moves through a congregation in much the way a Slinky moves. Play a bit with that coiled children's toy, and you'll learn a lot about how change moves through a congregation or any other organization. If you lift the top ring an inch

---

People adopt new ideas at different rates, and only as they are influenced by people they trust.

---

or two, you'll notice that only the next two or three coils are affected. The bulk of the Slinky stays put, exerting a pull on those leading rings to rejoin the main group.

Each ring in a Slinky moves only as a result of movement in the rings on either side. The first ring moves, stretching the ring next to it. If that second ring yields to the stretching and moves, then a third ring is stretched. If that third ring yields and moves, only then will the impetus to move reach the fourth ring. The Slinky arrives in a new location only after each ring has been moved by the influence of its neighbor.

A Slinky does not move into a new position all at once. Neither does a congregation. When one end of a Slinky starts slowly to move, the movement further down the coil is tentative, as if the rings were unsure whether to stay or go. People move in their own time and only after the individuals they most respect have moved. This movement often has a testing quality. The decision to move forward can be followed by a hasty retreat. One definition of leadership is the ability to influence people toward a particular end or result. When it comes to congregational change, every person in the congregation is a leader. Every person has a ring of influence, whether or not he or she is aware of it.

Those who initiate change or become early leaders of renewal face temptations in two directions. "Should we wait for the consensus of the congregation before we start anything, or should we simply plow ahead full speed?" Neither choice will help the congregation move. A Slinky can move only if the first ring moves. Waiting for full consensus of the congregation before taking a first step guarantees that the step will never be taken. On the other hand, moving too fast can leave the next ring of people feeling rushed and pressured. When people feel forced, their natural response is to resist.

Jerry, the lay leader of a Lutheran congregation, related that after six months of prayer and study, the renewal team members had reached a clear and common understanding of the mission

Lasting change happens as people are drawn forward by purpose, vision, and values—not by being forced.

of their congregation. The team summarized it in a concise statement, which was handed out to various leaders of teams and committees, so that all the work of the congregation could be aligned to meet the aim. The renewal team was surprised and frustrated that nothing happened. The team forgot that its new understanding of and enthusiasm for the congregation's mission came as a result of those six months of prayerful study. It tried to yank the next ring of leadership up, rather than creating settings where those leaders could think about, contribute to, test out, and finally claim for themselves a new way of being and doing church.

Using scare tactics or pointing to dire consequences to motivate change doesn't work either, and verges on manipulation. Threats may initially provoke movement, but they cannot sustain it. Change made as a result of being pushed, shamed, or "guilted" generally reverses itself as soon as pressure is removed.

Lasting change happens as people are drawn forward by purpose, vision, and values, deciding for themselves that the shift is beneficial and worthwhile. Hearing others speak about "why this is important to me" provides helpful information to people reflecting on that question for themselves. Gradually, the Slinky moves—a few links at a time.

People Will Ask the Same Four Questions— Over and Over

Organizational consultant William Bridges, writing on the topic of change and transition, points out the distinction between the two. Change is a shift from one situation to another. We

Change is a shift from one situation to another. Transition is the internal process we go through to adapt to that change.

change clothes. We change jobs. We change homes. Transition is the internal process a person goes through to come to terms with a change. Janice's new home seemed odd to her at first. She couldn't remember where she put things, and it smelled, well, *different*. At times she even found herself taking the wrong freeway exit and heading toward her old apartment. A year later, none of those things were true; she felt that her home was indeed *her* home. Transition is the work of settling into a new normal. The more a change affects patterns and practices we hold dear, the more difficult the transition. This principle is especially valid when the change is not self-imposed.

Moving into a new home is usually a change we impose upon ourselves after carefully thinking through some key questions. We believe there's a good reason for the move. We form a mental picture of how we'll feel living in the new home, and how the home will look. We've figured out a plan for moving out of the home where we now live and into the new one. We believe that we can make new friends and ultimately feel at home there. All those mental preparations induce us to take on the work of packing up, saying good-bye, learning the intricacies of a new home, and making new friends.

But often change is imposed upon us. Unless we see a good reason for it, the natural first response is resistance. The majority of people in your congregation will experience congregational change this way. Reasonably satisfied with their church experience, they may see little reason for change. Members will resist making the needed transitions unless they are convinced that there's a good reason for changing what they think already works well enough. When pushed, they'll challenge the changes, asking such questions as "What's the problem with the way things are?" and "Who says we need to change, and how do they know?"

Bridges's research says that people being asked to adapt to new ways of thinking and behaving need answers about four aspects of the intended change—purpose, picture, plan, and place. Here are his four P's:

- What's the *purpose* of doing this?

- What's the *picture* of what this will look like and feel like for the people?

- What's the *plan* for getting there?

- Will there be a *place* for me . . . what part will I play?

We've found that people are usually more concerned with one "P" than the others, but which one varies with the individual. Some will need to understand why the changes are necessary. Some, before they can give their support, will need to be able to envision the outcome and to imagine how they would feel being part of the renewed congregation. Once they get a picture in their heads and a vision in their hearts, they trust that the way to get there will be found. Others are more pragmatic. They find the picture interesting, but their real questions revolve around practical issues: "So how do we do it? Who's going to do the work? Where's the funding coming from?" Others, knowing that shifts in a congregation's culture often lead to shifts in leadership and in who does what, are concerned about their future role in the congregation. Those invested in particular ministries and programs may wonder if there will be any place for them after the changes. This concern, even more than the others, raises anxiety in people and leaves them feeling threatened.

You'll hear these four questions raised in various ways throughout the process. When individuals begin to feel themselves stretched by new ideas and practices, they start questioning.

When people complain or make challenging comments, listen for whether they're really asking questions about Bridges's four P's: purpose, picture, plan, and place.

Leaders who answered these questions for themselves long ago may tire of answering the same questions over and over again for others. To make matters more challenging, often these questions are not posed in a straightforward way.

If people feel threatened by the proposed changes, their questions will often take the form of complaints or challenges. At a church meeting, an older woman announced frostily, "Only children and young families count here anymore. It's clear that the older adults, the ones who built this church, are not welcome or wanted." Her aggressive tone, offensive to many in the room, masked deeper questions: In her growing and changing congregation, was there still a place for her and those like her? Was she still a wanted and needed member of her beloved church community?

It's easy to respond to the words or the tone of voice and miss the deeper questions raised. When people complain or make challenging comments, listen for whether one of the four questions is at the heart of the matter. Don't get rattled by complaints or obsess over them. As much as possible, hold the perspective that this reaction is feedback from congregation members about what they need from leaders if they are to make the needed transition. Recognizing the deeper issues that drive members' complaints helps leaders understand how best to respond and provide appropriate leadership.

When introducing new ideas or proposing changes, Bridges's four P's can help you think through what people need to know. Are we clear about the purpose for these changes, the larger results we want for the congregation? Can we explain it in plain and simple language that people understand? Can we describe the hoped-for results? Are we communicating the plan clearly enough? Have we left out important details? Are people feeling left out or left behind?

Remember, too, that if you want people to grasp what you're trying to communicate, they will need to hear it multiple times and in a variety of ways. We tend to blame people when they don't hear the message. Usually, the failure is ours. We've not expressed the message in a form they take much notice of. We've buried it under an avalanche of other information. We've said it once, thinking that would be enough. We've said it at a time when people's attention was elsewhere. Communicate, communicate, and communicate. If you're not absolutely sick of trying to get the message out to the congregation about purpose, picture, plan, and each member's place in everything you do and in every place you go, you have not communicated enough.

Conflict Is Inevitable

If no one has told you before, we want you to hear it now: shifting the culture of a congregation generates conflict—significant conflict. Some of the conflict will make sense to you; you'll see it coming. But if your congregation is typical, at some point you'll be blindsided by conflict that seems to arise from nowhere and to leave you wondering whether your congregation can survive it.

Conflict arises when people perceive a threat to their needs, interests, concerns, or values. It's the sense of threat that causes the problems. When people feel that they stand to lose something deeply important, they not only resist—they fight. Congregational renewal requires people to make significant shifts in their practices and their thinking about their church, their community, and their relationship with God. People naturally wonder and worry about how these shifts may compromise what they hold to be most important about their congregation.

Most people truly love their church and may resist or even fight when what they cherish seems threatened.

Those satisfied with the status quo may find the very idea of renewal threatening. Others will agree with the concept but reject the reality of change. "We explained over and over what the plan was and what it would entail," said a board member of a small California church as she shook her head in confusion. "The congregation approved it unanimously, and we called a pastor based on that plan. But now that he's here and we're actually addressing these things, all hell has broken loose. I've lost count of the times people have said, 'Yes, I voted for it, but I didn't know it meant *that*.'"

Many churchgoers seem to have the idea that Christians are always supposed to "be nice" and are never to disagree with one another at church, so they don't share openly their differing viewpoints. Members "stuff" their frustration until it leaks out or boils over. At that point, four destructive attitudes typically arise: blame, defensiveness, contempt, and stonewalling (refusal to respond). Relationship researcher John Gottman calls these attitudes the four horsemen of the apocalypse, because of their ability to stymie connection and creativity. When one of these shows up in a group, the others generally ride out to meet it.

Blame, defensiveness, contempt, and stonewalling are natural reactions by which we protect ourselves when we feel threatened. In renewal, you're making significant shifts to the community where people have found meaning and have experienced belonging. Members have married or seen their children marry at the altar rail, brought children and grandchildren to be baptized, and mourned the passing of loved ones. Simply stepping into the building evokes memories of significant moments in their lives. The people in your congregation have attachments to particular traditions, practices, and routines; these are venues in which they have experienced God. Those facing significant change in other aspects of their lives may feel overwhelmed at the thought that their congregation is changing, too. We often hear some form of the phrase, "I need my church to be the one place that doesn't change." When changes begin to take place, even much-desired changes, the climate can become highly charged emotionally.

Most congregations avoid conflict at all costs. They swing between putting lids on disagreements and cleaning up messes after the contained pot boils over. A congregation's discomfort with conflict can lead it to back away from renewal when serious disagreements arise. Leaders don't know what else to do; they believe that going forward might split or even kill the congregation.

Conflict causes problems primarily because people don't know what to do with all the energy generated when people voice divergent opinions about issues they care about. That's a definition of conflict we've heard several conflict specialists offer—two or more divergent ideas bumping up against each other. We like it. It reminds us that conflict isn't the enemy but a natural part of the renewal process as new ideas arise about how to be and do church. The problem lies in how we respond when our deeply held conviction bumps up against someone else's very different one. Generally, emotions rise, and either we tense up or shut down. If we can stay open and curious, even as we experience discomfort, conflict gives us more ideas to work with and unleashes tremendous energy.

When managed skillfully, conflict wakes people up, provokes new lines of thinking, and provides energy. Surfacing differing positions and ideas creates the pool that spawns new thoughts, new ideas, and unexpected growth. Addressed early and well,

---

Conflict is a natural part of the creative process.
Learn how to be present and work creatively with it.

Leaders influence people toward a particular end or result.

---

conflict can open the way for God to help something new happen in your midst. Learn how to be present with and work appreciatively with conflict. As a leader in your church, make it a priority to help your congregation develop skills in managing and using conflict.

Leaders Must Lead

Even though the work of renewal belongs to the people of the congregation, the work cannot be done without leadership, great leadership. Leaders tend to the alliance and alignment of a congregation. By alliance, we mean the capacity of the members of the congregation to get along, the quality of their relationships, and their ability to embody Christian community. By alignment we mean the degree to which members and groups agree about the congregation's purpose and goals. People can get along well but never accomplish much because they're working at cross-purposes. Likewise, they can achieve great results but do so in a way that leaves people feeling angry and marginalized. A strong congregation helps people develop healthy, life-giving relationships as they link their gifts and interests in developing and achieving goals that matter to them.

During renewal, your congregation's leaders must directly address the alignment and alliance of the congregation as they help the group move step by step along the renewal path. If the members are to follow, leaders must influence people toward a particular end or result. They do this through both their *being* and their *doing*.

"Being" refers to embodying the qualities that help people trust and follow. These inner qualities are components and reflections of the leaders' own spiritual and emotional health. While many qualities of "being" are important, we lift up five as foundational for those leading congregational renewal. Leaders must be anchored in these and embody them.

- *Faith*: Leaders stay attuned to God's presence, listen for God's leading, and believe that faithful work faithfully done will ultimately yield the fruit God desires.

- *Trust*: Leaders trust themselves, and they trust others.

- *Compassion*: Leaders commit to be "with" people in their feelings and experiences, connecting with them heart to heart.

- *Differentiation*: Leaders are aware of where their own life and work start and stop, and where someone else's begins.

- *Mindfulness*: Leaders are awake and attentive to the present moment—themselves and their impact, others, the world, and the interaction of people. They meet each moment with an eye to the bigger aims and scope of life: past, present, and future.

The "doing" of leadership describes the basic actions of a leader, no matter what specific endeavor he or she is engaged in. We lift up five activities that are essential.

- *Envisioning*: Leaders develop and hold for themselves and others a picture of the desired future. They help people understand how their present work contributes to the ultimate aims.

- *Articulating:* Leaders frame and reframe the church's story. They tell the story so that it makes sense of the past,

---

Leaders give themselves full permission to take risks. They assume full responsibility for the impact of their actions.

---

names the reality and meaning of the present, and points to the next chapter of the congregation's God-story.

- *Orchestrating:* Leaders bring people and their gifts together, encouraging and organizing the people to interact in such a way that they link minds, hearts, and hands to determine and accomplish worthy objectives.

- *Improvising:* Leaders creatively adjust, weaving and re-weaving, bringing together seemingly disparate strands in service of the bigger goals.

- *Embodying:* This final activity combines both being and doing as leaders "walk the talk," maintaining a congruency between their values, their words, and their behavior.

These qualities and activities are the basis for skilled group facilitation. But leaders are more than facilitators helping people determine and carry out an agenda. Leaders have opinions. They set a group's basic agenda. Leaders of congregational renewal need to have an opinion about the best direction for the congregation and to keep that agenda before the people. They must have a deep investment in the people's discerning and following God's call. Leaders act with boldness and courage for the sake of achieving a better future for the congregation. They give themselves full permission to take risks. At the same time, leaders need to watch for and take responsibility for the impact of their decisions and actions. Trying new things and taking risks will occasionally create messes. Good leaders are quick to take responsibility for cleaning up those messes. They accept full permission and full responsibility—all in the service of the congregation's call.

Clergy and lay leaders in a congregation engaged in renewal must function on two tracks. On one track they are maintaining, and at times improving, the existing organization and essential programs. On the other track they are creating something brand new. Leaders need continually to make decisions about where to focus attention among the existing programs, activities, and traditions. Some are nurtured. Some are left on their own either to make it or to die slowly. Some are intentionally stopped for the sake of freeing up financial, physical, and human resources for what is being created. Leaders maintain compassion for the people who are feeling losses. At the same time, however, they say no to the many small pulls that would consume the time and resources needed by the bigger aim to which they and the congregation have said yes.

Renewal Follows a Predictable Path, But the Right Step Is Situational

In many ways, congregational renewal is a known entity. We know what helps and what gets in the way. We know what to expect at certain points. And we know that certain work must be solidly in place for further work to be useful. On the other hand, every congregation's experience on that journey is different. Each congregation must discern the timing and the manner for moving through those steps. The work must be tailored to that particular group of people in that location, at that point in their congregation's life.

Principles of congregational renewal and the overall pathway remain the same from congregation to congregation. However, practices (how those principles are lived out) do not always translate well from one congregation to another. What worked beautifully for one congregation may flop for another. A resource one congregation finds trivial and poorly designed may be exactly what another finds most helpful. Replicating the

Beware of copying what others have done. Develop the ability instead to listen for, discern, and respond to God's calling.

solutions of others can be a dangerous shortcut. It keeps the congregation and its leaders from acquiring the strengths and capabilities that are developed during renewal. It may even lead you to a place where you didn't intend to go!

Much of the formation of a congregation happens as the people struggle together to determine the practices that will best serve their forward movement. A congregation and its leaders learn continually to ask, "Given the future we feel God calling us to and what is true for us right now, what is the best way to proceed? What is the best way for us to take this next step?" This work requires a congregation to develop the ability to listen for, discern, and respond to God's calling.

Don't put your faith in a detailed blueprint that someone hands you. Nor should you expect to create in advance every detail of your own plan. Transformation will take place as people give themselves to each other, to those beyond the church, and to God. Nothing can take the place of people sitting and talking, being open and curious with one another, creating together. Plan, yes—but be prepared to change and adjust those plans. You will build the bridge to your future even as you are walking across it. Renewal is absolutely a journey of faith.

At times, the process will seem to stall, and renewal will not progress at the pace you anticipated. This stalling may be simply a matter of timing. There is no definitive timetable. Step back and ask these questions: Do we still believe we're taking the right next step? Is there an in-between step we've missed? Or are we taking the right step but not in the right way? Or do we all simply need to be a bit more patient? Learning to ask those questions and to answer them accurately is one of the great benefits of renewal.

Your congregation is not the first to walk this path. The experiences of other congregations can be enlightening and helpful. Talk to others. Learn from their experience, but walk your own road. Resist the temptation to copy other congregations' journeys. The right way for your congregation to address each step depends on the many factors unique to your congregation. The work of discerning the right way for your congregation to address a step is as important as taking the step itself.

An Unfortunate Truth

Most congregations end up staying on their original trajectory. Many say that they want renewal. Many take steps in that direction. Some even invest significant amounts of money into the work, attending workshops or bringing in a consultant to help them. Yet very few congregations see the work through to the end.

A primary factor is the enormous gravitational pull of the existing system and its ingrained patterns. Two steps forward are all too often followed by two steps backward, without our even realizing it's happening. We call this oft-seen movement *oscillation*. We experience oscillation in many facets of our personal lives. Weight loss is a good example. We become dissatisfied with our weight or our health, and we want things to be different. We take steps and, experiencing the desired change, settle into enjoying the improvement. And then one day we wake up and realize that we've gained all the weight back, and we start the cycle again. Oscillation happens because we underestimate the lure of familiar patterns and their powerful influence.

Congregations tend to declare victory too soon. Life together will have a different appearance and texture long before the activities that moved the congregation to that point have become ingrained patterns. Weight-loss experts now say that diets don't work; what's needed is changed habits of eating and exercise. Renewal can be viewed in the same way. It's less of an effort to reach a particular point than it is to develop a new way of thinking about and doing church. Congregations that declare the work finished once they reach the point at which life feels good will fail to develop the habits that will keep the congregation there.

Congregations revert to their former ways also because the personal cost of change becomes simply too great. People begin to recognize that continuing forward with renewal will likely mean abandoning cherished practices, much-loved traditions, and familiar patterns of worship, work, and fellowship. They feel torn by competing commitments. Even though they had good intentions and had declared a commitment to give themselves to renewal of their congregation, people find themselves unwilling to let go of the congregation as it is. That inability to say *no* to the old leads them to being unwilling to say *yes* to the new. They see the new displacing what they value, and they are not willing to pay the cost.

Another factor that leads congregations to abandon renewal is people's loss of trust—in themselves, in others, and even in God. Seeing how impossibly huge the work of renewal is, they begin to focus on the word "impossible." They imagine themselves unable to do what is called for. Losing confidence in themselves, they also begin to lose confidence in the abilities of others. And finally, they begin to forget what God can do with five loaves and two fish.

We find that the loss of both will and trust arises particularly in congregations that fail to spend time cultivating their individual and communal relationships with God. Congregational renewal cannot progress without the congregation's becoming and staying anchored in what God desires for the world and for the church. Without that anchoring, people declare victory as soon as enough progress has been made to satisfy their own needs. Or they turn back when they feel that what is most important to them is being threatened. Their focus will be what they want in the moment rather than what God wants in the long term.

A Word of Hope

Having alerted you to some key challenges and to the sad fact that the majority of congregations never move off their old trajectory, we want you also to know that renewal is possible. It's taking place in large and small congregations, in dwindling rural communities, and in urban centers that are burgeoning. Renewal is possible. We've talked with pastors and lay leaders across the United States and Canada who are finding a new heart for God and a new passion for ministry. Some of them serve congregations that their judicatories had all but given up on. A surprising number are congregations too small to afford a full-time or ordained clergy leader.

What makes the difference? As far as we can tell, it's the people—how much they want a new future and whether they're willing to take responsibility for creating it. God is the great "I Am," present in every moment, waiting for us to notice and to respond. We can remember and honor the past. We can dream about the future. But we can think and act and *live* only in the present moment. Only by acting in the here-and-now do we experience God and create God's kin-dom.

Hold in your heart memories of moments when the church was really "being church." Dream of the difference it would make for you, and for others like you, if that memory described the normal state of your congregation. Renewal happens as you make a habit of living that new life, now. Don't ever underestimate your power to effect change. Congregations shift member by member. Live renewal. Live it each and every day. That's what makes the difference.

Discussion Questions

Take the time to discuss the following questions with others in your congregation.

1. Which of the "challenges" were new to you? Which one surprised you the most? Why?

2. The authors say they've "never seen a congregation shift its culture in a lasting way in less than seven years." What would you and the congregation need in order to stay focused on a task (renewal) for that length of time?

3. Where in the congregation or beyond have you seen the "Slinky principle" at work?

4. Think about the disagreements that have arisen in your congregation. What is your congregation's typical way of handling conflict?

5. Think back to a moment when a substantial change was pending in your congregation. Which of Bridges's four questions did you yourself most need to have answered to reach a decision?

6. Read back through the list of leaders' qualities of "being" and "doing." Which comes most easily for you? Which is most difficult? Which seems confusing?

7. Recall an instance in your current or a previous congregation's past when it listened for, discerned, and responded to God's calling. What was that experience like?

8. As you reflect on why congregations give up their efforts toward renewal, which temptation do you think will be strongest for your congregation? What might help the congregation continue to move forward when that temptation arises?

3
Developing Readiness
PREPARING THE LEADERS TO LEAD

This chapter looks at the first work facing a congregation in need of renewal—developing readiness. Envisioning and planning receive most of the attention in discussions about renewal. But until a congregation's leaders are ready and committed to lead along a new path, little will change. This first phase of work prepares leaders to guide the congregation in a new direction. The ultimate aim of this phase is for the formal leaders to reach the point at which they:

- believe the congregation's current trajectory is unacceptable

- have a basic idea and some experience of how a renewed congregation would differ from the congregation's current reality

- are committed to do whatever it takes to lead the congregation into a renewed experience and expression of church

When leaders don't reject the current path of the congregation, they never give themselves fully to a new vision. Instead, they subtly but surely bend any new vision to fit within the boundaries of current patterns. Developing a basic understanding of what renewal is, and an experience and appreciation of this different way of being church, provokes leaders to want

Until a congregation's leaders want a renewed
congregation and are committed to lead in that
direction, little will change.

something new for their congregation and to create settings
where others can learn and grow. However, it takes courage
and perseverance to provide the needed leadership. Chaos and
conflict go hand in hand with renewal as new ideas challenge
established patterns and ways of thinking. Leaders must truly
want a renewed congregation and must be committed to helping it happen.

Congregations that skip this work of developing readiness
in the congregation's leaders, or attend to it in only a cursory
fashion, find that they never make much progress. In order for
envisioning and planning to lead to a new way of living and
working together, this preliminary work must be done. Ignoring "readiness work" causes renewal efforts to stall or fail. Your
congregation's leaders must develop urgency, commitment,
and focus to lead the congregation successfully along the path
of renewal. The steps of phase 1 develop these qualities in a
congregation's leaders. Even more important, these steps foster
personal renewal. This renewal of heart, mind, and spirit is the
essence of congregational renewal. A congregation will go no
further and no deeper than its leaders.

As you read this chapter, you may discover that your congregation has already done some, or perhaps all, of the work of
developing readiness. If that is the case, congratulations! Use
this chapter to deepen your understanding and appreciation for
what's been accomplished. We'll be speaking here as if your
congregation is just beginning its work. We want you to see the
full scope of this phase so that you can spot any areas where further work may need to be done. You're ready to begin surfacing
a guiding vision of a renewed congregation when the formal

leaders of your congregation are of one mind: "Where we are or where we're heading is unacceptable, and we are determined to provide the needed leadership for our congregation to truly be church, the body of Christ in the world, for the world."

For leaders to reach the decision that the congregation's current trajectory is unacceptable, several things must happen. Leaders need to develop a shared understanding of the mission and purpose of God's church. They must be able to answer these questions: "What is the purpose of the church? What Scriptures are foundational to our understanding of what a congregation is supposed to be and do? What are the unique denominational understandings of our work?" Leaders then need to educate themselves about the current nature of their congregation and the community in which it's situated. What impact does congregational life have on the members? What impact does the congregation have on its surrounding community? These two areas of exploration provide clergy and lay leaders with the information they need to project the likely outcomes in five to ten years if the congregation continues on its current course. If they conclude that the congregation needs to shift directions, leaders must be willing to lead. Effective leaders do what needs to be done for the sake of the transformation of the congregation and the differences that will be made in people's lives because of that transformation.

At times this commitment will require leaders to take stands unpopular with many of the congregation's members. The Exodus story tells of the Hebrew people's forty-year journey from captivity in Egypt to the promised land. The story begins not with the people's traveling, but with their being locked into a life of slavery that promised no better future. In the beginning, the Hebrew supervisors saw Moses's actions as only worsening their situation. Moses's and Aaron's first meeting with Pharaoh resulted in an increased workload for the Israelites. The supply of straw with which the people made bricks was withheld, forcing the people to scatter across Egypt to gather the needed material.

Coming across Moses and Aaron, the Israelite supervisors furiously cried, "The LORD look upon you and judge! You have brought us into bad odor with Pharaoh and his officials, and have put a sword in their hands to kill us" (Exod. 5:21). We are not told what the people thought about their newly worsened conditions and these two seemingly self-appointed leaders, but we can imagine that those who knew the story agreed with the supervisors.

Scripture tells us how Pharaoh's heart was finally changed, but not how the hearts and minds of the supervisors and the rest of the Hebrew people were transformed. All we know is that when the time came for the people to pick up and move, "six hundred thousand men on foot, besides children," journeyed from Rameses to Succoth. "A mixed crowd also went up with them, and livestock in great numbers, both flocks and herds" (Exod. 12:37–38). It appears that somewhere along the line, a substantial number of people changed their minds about which future they would give themselves to. That shift in mental perspective enabled their physical journey. The very real journey that awaits your congregation is first a journey of hearts and minds. This inner journey requires no less determination and preparation than that required of the Hebrew people. And just as their journey began with Moses's and Aaron's transformation in thinking, your congregation's journey begins with the renewal of the hearts and minds of its leaders.

For a congregation to pick up and move in a dramatically different direction, its leaders must be committed to the change and able to organize and mobilize the people. To have credibility with the congregation, leaders must be willing to go first, to experience what they're asking others to experience, and to model the behavior they say is important. And who are those leaders? They're likely some of the very people who now provide leadership within your congregation. These leaders may also include people who, up until now, have *not* served in a leadership role.

The Initial Leaders

Your congregation already has leaders, people charged by the congregation with making decisions that serve the best interests of the congregation and its mission. Any organization that's been around for a while has developed norms for how work gets down and who does what. Systems theory says that when people come together for a purpose, the resulting group becomes a living, growing entity with its own unique personality and preferences. A group is flexible and spontaneous in its early years. As it ages, patterns develop, providing stability. But over time, these patterns codify and the group becomes pattern-dependent. New ideas, new behavior, and new ways of relating are seen as *interesting* at best. They and the people bringing them are nudged into compliance with the group's established norms.

Members newly elected to leadership positions pick up these norms as they serve in their new roles. In short order, and often without any verbal instruction, they absorb the habits and fall into the patterns of the existing group. A group's inherent power to bring an individual's behavior into line with the group's norms is called *entrainment*. We liken this power to a gravitational pull. A person may step into leadership with the full intent of doing things differently, but before long, his or her way of working and relating begins to take on the characteristics of the established group. Congregational renewal seeks to set new norms and ultimately to break the old patterns and the pattern-dependency of the congregational system. This shift is best initiated by a group of people that doesn't already formally exist. While the existing, overarching norms of the congregation will still be powerful, a new grouping of people has an easier time in establishing new norms. We call the new group that is needed a "germination group."

This germination group serves as the initial container for nurturing renewal. Its aim is to initiate new patterns of thinking, working, and relating. This first small group of interested

---

A germination group brings together interested people to have initial conversations about a different way of being and doing church.

---

people come together to learn and talk with each other about renewal, to dream about what might be possible for their congregation, and to begin working toward a way of being with each other that more closely resembles the church of their dreams. This is their only task. This single focus makes it hard for an existing group to take on the work of renewal. Not only does an existing group have established norms; it has other work to attend to when it gathers. Boards that try to add renewal to their list of responsibilities find it taking a backseat to regular business and the crises that erupt periodically.

Gathering a Germination Group

Often this germination group is very small, initially just a few people who, with the pastor, share a longing for a different way of being and doing church. Usually it begins with one person speaking to another person. This conversation is more than just talk that "someone ought to do something." It is more than just "complaining." While it contains an element of dissatisfaction with current life in the congregation, it also includes a sense that something more is possible. It expresses a longing for more and a willingness to become involved.

What that "something more" is may not be clear. What's important is the desire for change and the willingness to take part. Sometimes it's the pastor who starts the process. Sometimes a layperson provides the impetus. Sometimes it's a collective "aha!" in a committee or other small-group meeting. Gathering a germination group is like finding and bringing together warm embers that can get the fire going.

This group cannot be formed by legislation. It requires a certain chemistry between the members. So, if your first attempts fall flat, don't give up. Look for individuals who want something more for their congregation and community, who are willing to spend some time and energy in conversation, and who are open to stretching and growing personally. As your group of two or three talk, begin to think of others whom you want to invite into the conversation. What we've found across the board is that for the group to be effective, it must include both pastor and laity.

While the pastor may not initiate the movement toward renewal, he or she must become involved at this early stage if renewal is to take hold. The pastor cannot make renewal happen, but his or her "no" can certainly stop the process. Renewal requires a partnership between the congregation's laity and clergy. In many instances, the roles of each and the relationship between the two are part of what needs realigning. The germination group is the ideal place to begin.

You will likely find it helpful for some of the lay members of the germination group to be part of the formal leadership of the congregation. This informal exploration by a few people will eventually need to make a transition, becoming an official endeavor authorized by the congregation's governing board. Having people in place on the board makes this transition easier and, at the same time, provides a natural avenue for the "yeast" of the germination group to come in contact with the official structures of the congregation.

It takes time and intention to surface the right people. This step does not happen without effort. Offering targeted short-term learning opportunities can help to surface interested people.

Renewal begins simply, with two or three people having conversations about what might be possible.

Consider inviting likely people to gather in a home to read and discuss a book on renewal or to engage in a series of conversations about renewal. The idea is to create opportunities for people to explore their hopes for the congregation and to see if they find within themselves a calling to the work.

At mid-sized West Hill United Methodist Church, Pastor George made a point of sitting at the local Starbucks early on Saturday mornings to think about the congregation and to watch the neighborhood wake up. He invited various congregational leaders to join him. Across six months a small but regular group emerged. On any given Saturday morning at seven, you'd find George and two or three others drinking coffee, watching people, and talking deeply about the future of their congregation.

The germination group started much differently at smaller Parker First Church. At forty-seven, Terry had served in almost every congregational leadership role at one time or another. He ached for something more for his congregation but was at a loss as to what to do. The previous pastors had been kind and well intentioned, but the congregation had continued to decline. When Pastor Sandra arrived, Terry watched and listened for many months. Sensing she would understand and be able to help, he approached her. "I want to learn about how churches grow and how I can help that happen here," he said. In this congregation, renewal began with these two interested people reading books and sharing their learning and questions with one another.

Part of the work in this early stage involves fostering a sense of both community and responsibility among those in the group. The beginning of renewal within a congregation is similar to a community organizer's work in starting a movement. A movement begins when people's dissatisfaction with the current situation and where it might lead is linked with a keen desire for what could be. Rooted in both dissatisfaction and desire, a movement grows as people discover and create a pathway to a different future. In starting renewal, you are not

The germination group provides a setting where people can experience church in a new way.

mounting a campaign but starting a movement. Your ultimate aim is to form an ever-growing group of passionate and committed people, working together, to change the culture from the inside out.

The goal of renewal is a congregation that notices and experiences God in its midst; that seeks to align its efforts with God's will; and that, finding that kind of life beneficial, extends it to others. Right from the start then, gatherings need to be more than meetings. The idea is for the people in this germination group to experience something different, something compelling, and to learn to take responsibility for creating the kind of community they're experiencing. These shifts happen not through a book the group may read, but through the relationships they form with each other and with God as they discuss that book or join in conversation.

In our book *Practicing Right Relationship*, we explore how conscious and intentionally "right" relationships transform individuals and the systems of which they are a part:

By "right" we don't mean "right and wrong." The word in this context refers to being in an appropriate, healthy, or God-intended position in relationship to others. In God's vision for creation, people relate to each other in particular ways. These relationships are characterized by honor, respect, love, and care. Right relationships are creative, mutual, and generative; life-giving things are birthed. When we are in right relationship, we embody these God-intended ways of being with each other. Righting a tipped-over vase restores its functionality. Righting our relationships restores the fullness of their functionality as well (*Practicing Right Relationship*, p. 7).

Each step of the renewal journey includes both external and internal work that must be done. The external focus of the group is the renewed congregation it wants to create. This desire for a renewed congregation provides the future goal for the germination group and for all the successive groups that will lead the congregation toward renewal. This common purpose shifts the group from being a collection of individuals with multiple aims to being a unified body with a common focus. People are committed to something bigger than themselves and their own interests. The external work of the germinating group is dreaming together about what might be possible for the congregation.

To move toward that alternate future, the group must practice a new way of being community. This is the internal work of the group. It focuses on altering the group members' relationships with one another and with God.

Changing how congregation members relate to one another can be challenging. Often, they've known each other for years. And knowing each other so well, they no longer really see one another. Once we've experienced or observed a person, we tend to cast him or her in a role. Categorizing is a natural human response. It allows us to decide instantly how to relate and respond to a person. When we give someone a label, we tend to base our interactions with them on that role. Once we start thinking of Sally as a "difficult person," it's hard to see her actions through any other lens or to relate to her in any other way. It can be hard to let go of the stories we've made up about people. In a congregation with long-standing relationships, the patterns of how people relate to one another are deeply ingrained.

Just as ingrained are the patterns people develop, both individually and as a congregation, for relating to God. Being in right relationship with God means being open to having our hearts and minds continually transformed. We allow our attitudes and thoughts toward our neighbor and the world to be formed by the attitudes and thoughts of Christ. The hard-

Renewal depends on people learning to be open, authentic, caring, and curious with each other and with God.

est work facing the germination group, each of the successive groups that will provide leadership, and the congregation itself is learning to be open, authentic, caring, and curious with each other and with God. This attitude is what transforms people and what ultimately transforms a congregation.

Enlarging the Germination Group

Just as the germination group settles into a comfortable pattern for itself, it's time for the group to change what it has come to know and love. For renewal to take hold, the tiny germination group must expand. It must relinquish its ownership of the process and welcome others in. This shift can be a challenge. The group will face the same temptation of clinging to a fulfilling experience that Peter, James, and John faced when they were with Jesus at the time of the transfiguration: "Lord, it is good for us to be here; if you wish, I will make three dwellings here, one for you, one for Moses, and one for Elijah" (Matt. 17:4). The group will likely have had fulfilling experiences together. The group members will relish the feelings of community, satisfaction, and fulfillment. They may even be afraid that others will "ruin" the group. The germination group must trust God enough to let go of what is good, so that God can bring something even better. This is the challenge ultimately facing the entire congregation.

There is no hard-and-fast rule about the right time or the right way to expand the group. The germination group needs to have been together long enough to form an identity and norms that honor the best of the current congregation and stand in contrast to its worst. The idea is to use the natural entrainment of systems to your advantage, establishing a new way of being and acting into which new members of the germination group feel drawn.

At Parker First, the enlargement happened quite naturally. One book in particular caught Terry's and Sandra's imaginations. Even before they'd finished reading it, Terry picked up the phone and called Sandra. "John needs to read this. This is exactly what he was saying the other day. What if I asked him to join us?"

"That's a great idea!" said Sandra. "Who else needs to be a part of reading this?" Together they came up with a list of ten people and invited them to gather on Sunday evenings at Terry's house for dessert and discussion. Very quickly, Sunday night became a much-anticipated part of the participants' week. Sylvia, an older, longtime member of the congregation, reflected, "I come away from these evenings feeling so close to people. And I'm so buzzing with ideas that I have a have hard time going to sleep!"

At West Hill, enlarging the group took more effort and thought. Members of the Saturday-morning group enjoyed their time together and didn't really want to give it up. At the same time, they knew that for the sake of the church, the conversation needed to include more people. Saturday morning wasn't going to work. Too many of the people they thought needed to be there had other commitments. It took the coffee group several weeks to figure out the best way to expand the conversation. In the end, the members identified four people they believed would add to the discussion. Two were key leaders in the congregation, and two were people newer to the church who embodied many of the qualities of the dreamed-of congregation.

Authorizing the Process

Once the idea of renewal captures the germination group's imagination, the question arises, "How do we formalize this process? How do we help renewal become an official endeavor of the church rather than the interest of just a few of us?" The germinating group must find a way to enroll the formal

Renewal must eventually shift from being the interest of a few to an officially sanctioned effort of the congregation.

leaders of the congregation, first to explore renewal and then to formally support a renewal effort within the congregation. This step further enlarges the circle of those exploring renewal and proclaims it an officially sanctioned effort of the congregation. Renewal, with its aim of realigning the life and work of a congregation, cannot take hold without the support of a congregation's formal leaders, clergy and lay.

For both the West Hill and Parker groups, this step was made easier in that well-respected key leaders were involved from the beginning. In addition, these people had not hidden their participation, but had been quite open with others about their appreciation for the gatherings they were part of and what they were learning. It did not come as a surprise to either congregation's governing board when a request was made to put a discussion about renewal on the board's agenda.

Each congregation has its own way of doing things, but in general it's not helpful to spring surprises on a board or decision-making group. We've seen instances when an informal group within the congregation did significant exploring and planning without the board's knowledge. The board was then asked to affirm the group's work and to change the direction of the congregation on the basis of a presentation that arose seemingly out of the blue. This approach generates resistance, distrust, and the use of the word "coup."

The point is not to usurp the governing board's role, but to honor it. Ideally, the handoff should go something like this: "We've been a part of an informal study group on congregational renewal. What we're learning and experiencing has us feeling hopeful about the future of the congregation. We're not sure where to go with it next, but we know that you as elected leaders, as the guiders of this church, are the right ones to determine if renewal is right for our congregation." Responsibility for the process must move out of the hands of the germination group and into the hands of a group that is granted official status. The congregation's governing board must guide this next step of the renewal process if renewal is to become an effort owned by the congregation and led by its leaders.

The group that carries renewal from this point through the rest of phase 1 has a very different job from that of the germination group. Formed by the congregation's governing board, this next group has the fundamental task of assessing the congregation's need for renewal. When people are asked to make a significant change, it is natural for them to ask, "Why? For what purpose? What's wrong with the way things are now?" The congregation's governing board will be responsible for leading renewal, a significant task that creates a good deal of conflict in a congregation. The board must be convinced that renewal is necessary to the long-term health of the congregation.

We find that this work is best done by either a subgroup of the board or a group appointed by the board. When taken on by the whole board, the work seems to get pushed aside in favor of ongoing business or new emergencies. Congregations that assign this work to a task force seem to move though the step more efficiently and effectively. The smaller size of the group and its formation as a new entity once again facilitates the development of new norms. We tend to refer to this group as the *renewal task force*. There's nothing magic in the name. It simply implies that the group is authorized by the board and asked to accomplish very specific tasks, and that it is different from the germination group.

This handoff of work from the germination group to the task force goes more smoothly when the task force includes many, if not the majority, of the germination group. Those who have already been thinking about renewal bring valuable perspectives and knowledge. They bring an already altered understanding of

The job of the renewal task force is to help the governing board assess the congregation's need for renewal.

what church can be, as well as patterns of relating that embody a sense of the renewed congregation. Don't assume though, that everyone who was part of the germination group will want to take part in this next phase of work. Those who loved the free-flowing conversation and dreaming may not want to take part in the nuts-and-bolts assessment work that dominates this step. That's fine. Those who step aside will continue to be yeast in the congregation, even if they are not directly involved in this aspect of renewal work. The relationships that were formed and the learning that took place will not be lost.

The task force, as a brand-new group, will take on its own personality and norms. Those with a history together must open themselves to what emerges as new people with new perspectives join the conversation and planning. This attitude of openness and flexibility tends to be lacking in a declining congregation, and it is needed for the congregation to let go of what its members know and to welcome something new.

If the membership of the task force duplicates the membership of an existing board or decision-making body, we strongly recommend that those meetings dealing with renewal be held at a different time and if at all possible in a different space. Sitting in the same room at the same table will make it difficult to establish new norms. Entrainment is that powerful! Consider meeting in the sanctuary, the narthex, a Sunday school room, or a home—anywhere that signals to everyone present that this work is not business as usual.

When first gathered in an unfamiliar setting, the members of an established group are initially awkward with each other. It's as if people suddenly aren't quite sure how to relate to one another if they're not sitting in their customary chairs. This moment of unease provides a golden opportunity. People don't like feeling awkward; they generally welcome direction that helps them know what's expected of them in this new setting. This is the time to try a new way of starting the gathering or running the meeting. It's a teachable moment, because the group has temporarily stopped functioning by rote. However, if the group is not guided in a new way of relating, the old patterns will quickly emerge, no matter how different the setting.

The Work of the Renewal Task Force

The renewal task force's job is to:

- educate itself about congregational renewal
- anchor itself in a biblical and denominational understanding of the purpose and aim of the church and congregation
- assess the current state of the congregation and its impact on its members and the surrounding community in relation to that purpose and aim
- bring to the board an assessment of the congregation's current trajectory and a recommendation about the congregation's future

The task force should provide the governing board with periodic updates on its work. These updates give the board the opportunity to ask questions and to stay current with what the task force is learning. Frequent reports prepare the board to work with and act on the recommendation the task force will ultimately bring. Keeping the board informed can lessen suspicion and resistance and provide the task force with helpful feedback. This feedback can alert the task force to issues it might have overlooked and spark insights that broaden the task force's perspective. Bringing periodic reports and learning from how they're received by the board also help the task force know better how to prepare and present its final recommendation. This information ensures that the report adequately addresses the questions that the board will likely raise.

This step is relatively brief, as the realities of a congregation and a community can change quickly. Whereas the germination phase may take a year or two, the task force should aim to complete its work in three to six months, with the bulk of the time being spent in the anchoring work discussed below. One task force, formed in June, completed its assessment work by October but didn't bring its formal report and recommendation until the following May. Since that report was not informed by the continuing shifts in the congregation, it didn't reflect the current reality. Your governing board needs current, accurate information to make a wise decision.

Learning about Congregational Renewal

The task force has been charged with exploring congregational renewal as a possible alternative to the congregation's current trajectory. To do this, the task force needs to understand what renewal is and what it entails. We suggest that the group study and discuss a book such as this one or one of those noted in our resource list. Talking with denominational staff well versed in congregational renewal can be helpful, too. The task force will need to help the governing board understand both the benefits and the challenges of renewal. Renewal is a long process that will ultimately bring up for examination every current practice of the congregation. While the idea of renewal is exciting and energizing, it's also hard work that demands a lot from the leaders and the people of a congregation. Congregational renewal is not something to jump into lightly. An important facet of the task force's role is educating the governing board about what it can expect if it chooses renewal. The task force starts by educating itself.

This initial time of studying together provides an ideal opportunity for the task force to develop a common understanding

---

The task force educates itself and the governing board on what can be expected if renewal is pursued.

---

of its task and good working relationships among its members. As the members learn together, those who were not part of the earlier germination group discussions have a chance to "catch up" and to inject their voices and opinions. For the task force, just as for the germination group, gatherings should be structured in ways that help the group be open, authentic, caring, and curious with each other and with God.

Developing a Common Understanding of the Purpose and Aim of the Church

The task force next reflects on the purpose of the church and the common hallmarks of a faithful congregation. Congregational change must be guided by principles larger than personal desires. Before they look to the future or make judgments about the present, the task force members must develop a solid and common basis for making their recommendations. This process requires the group to spend time immersing itself in Scripture, study, and prayer, continually asking, "What is the fundamental purpose of the church? What are the hallmarks of a faithful congregation? When is a congregation truly *being* church?"

Even if every member of the task force has a clear picture of the purpose and aim of the church and the work of a congregation, the group as a whole must develop a common understanding. This work orients the compass the group will use to determine the congregation's path. Studying together anchors the members and the group in the difference the church is supposed to make, and in a congregation's role in achieving that outcome.

This anchoring work is often skipped or performed in a cursory fashion. If it's an accepted practice in the congregation to start business meetings with a brief meditation and prayer, the group may bring that habit here and think that takes care of the anchoring work. This practice neither equips the group for the work ahead nor prepares participants to move beyond the entrained thinking of the congregation. A congregation truly in need of renewal is working off a faulty compass. Although it works hard, it never gets where it wants to go. The task force must establish trustworthy compass points.

You may find yourself in the position of many others, impatiently wanting to get on to the "real" work of assessment, and to crafting a recommendation. Know that nothing will serve that work more than giving yourself to study and reflection. Your task force's only job as it begins is to attend to its own education and formation. Appendix A gives suggestions for how your group can do this anchoring work. These practices engage the heart as well as the head. Ideally, all the work of the task force is done in a way that is formational for its members. The task force needs to structure its work in ways that help task force members experience generative relationships and an openness to God's leading.

We began working with the leadership team of Lewis United Presbyterian Church just after the renewal task force had been formed and commissioned. Already convinced that the church should give itself to all-out renewal, the group wanted the church to simply take a vote and get on with things. Why bother with all this preliminary stuff? "This church needs to change! It needs to grow!" Henry declared vehemently. Dan

Congregational change must be guided by principles larger than personal desires. Understanding the purpose of a Christian congregation and the difference it is supposed to make establishes the principles that will serve as trustworthy compass points.

nodded, asking, "I'm curious, Henry. What's your understanding of why it needs to grow?"

Henry was quick. "Because if we don't grow, this church will die, and I won't have this church to come to!" Heads nodded in agreement, but Henry blanched. Then he spoke again, very quietly: "Oh. That's not what church is supposed to be about, is it? It's absolutely what I want, but I'm pretty sure it's not supposed to be what we're aiming for—just ensuring that we have a place that can host our funerals when we die."

The group members decided they needed to spend some time clarifying their aims and anchoring themselves in a larger and more biblical vision of the purpose of the church. The task force invited the governing board to join it in prayer, Bible study, and conversation on four Saturday mornings. First, the participants studied, talked, and prayed in small groupings, and then they re-formed as one large group to share insights. The task force took the lead in these gatherings, and then met again on its own to reflect further on what people were learning about God's intentions for congregations.

The task force found that this early work with the governing board resulted in a common language and understanding that made later conversations with the board easier. The renewal task force at Lake Williams Presbyterian Church engaged in the work differently but with equal success. That group undertook a private twelve-week study that explored the overarching purpose of the church from various perspectives—biblical, denominational, and cultural.

However it is done, it is important that this anchoring work not result in a concrete vision. Remember, this is the *readiness* phase of renewal. The envisioning and planning phase comes later. The task force's role is one of reconnaissance. It does the preliminary fieldwork, establishing the initial compass points that will provide the basis for envisioning and guide subsequent planning.

Assessing Current Reality

Once the renewal task force has developed a shared understanding of the purpose and aim of the church and the hallmarks of a faithful congregation, its members are ready to
move on to their next task: assessing what's currently true
about their congregation and the surrounding community.
A group may think it has a clear picture of current reality,
but slow incremental changes tend to sneak up on people.
One woman commented, "I live in the community and have
attended this church for years. I was surprised how much I
didn't know about both! The congregation and neighborhood have really changed across the past fifteen years." Many
groups are surprised by what they find. Charged with bringing a recommendation, the task force must make sure that its
opinions are based in reality rather than in out-of-date information and personal assumptions and biases.

This is a time of collecting demographic information about
the neighborhood and statistical information about the congregation: Who lives in our area? What have been the changes
over the past ten years? What changes are projected for the
next ten? What are the primary challenges faced by the community right now? And what's true about our congregation?
What is the current worship attendance, and what has been
the trend over the past ten years? What's the financial situation? Who makes up our congregation? How many baptisms
do we have each year? Gil Rendle and Alice Mann's excellent book *Holy Conversations* offers processes in its resource
section that can help you learn about your congregation and
community.

In addition to these "hard" facts, the task force needs to reflect
on the quality of life within the congregation. What is it like to be
part of this congregation? What's the mood on Sunday morning?
What is it like to serve on committees here? What gets said in the
parking lot that doesn't get said within the walls of the church?
What do members say is the difference the congregation makes

When assessing current reality, the task force reflects on the quality of life within the congregation as well as on statistical data about the congregation and community.

in their lives? Much of this kind of information is best gathered through focus groups and interviews with members.

Resist the temptation to assign the gathering of information to one person. That approach results in one person's becoming the expert. We find that the work is easier and brings better results if it is divided among the entire team. The renewal task force at Lake Williams made a list of the information needed, broke it into themed categories, and then assigned each category to a team of two from the group. The teams had three months across the summer to do their work. The evening the task force formed the teams, it also set aside a day in early September for a retreat. At the retreat, each team would present its findings; then the group would discuss where its members saw the congregation heading.

Working in pairs kept the process moving. As September neared, the teams challenged each other to find interesting, creative, perhaps even playful ways to share what they'd learned. Their goal was to present the material in ways that would help people understand and remember it. The retreat began with group members listing on newsprint what they believed church should be about, drawing on what surfaced in their initial twelve weeks of study. They then moved to presenting their findings about the congregation and the neighborhood. They spent time in both prayer and conversation as they reflected on the congregation's future if life together continued in the same fashion.

Bringing a Formal Recommendation

The final task of the renewal task force is to bring a formal recommendation about the congregation's trajectory to the governing board. The task force has developed a sense of the overarching purpose and aim of the church and faithful congregations. It has gathered current and accurate information about the congregation and community. Now the group must project what will be true for the congregation in the future if its current way of living and working together remain the same. If the task force has found that path problematic, it outlines the possible character and outcome of a renewal path.

"Some people are still experiencing the considerable gifts of Lewis United—particularly our newest participants." This is how the report of the Lewis Task Force began.

> The newer people appreciate the warmth and sense of community they experience from the pastor and the people and the ability to be involved in practical service. One newer participant told us, "The people here are teaching me what it means to be of service. That's really important for me to learn." The majority of the congregation, however, is deeply frustrated. Having experienced a high level of "Lewis at its best" in the past, they are frustrated and upset with how little of that they experience now. They see the congregation shrinking in size and the average age of the people attending becoming older. As people leave, move away, or age, the work falls to a smaller pool of people. In general, people are feeling tired, frustrated, angry, and hurt, and don't know how to talk openly to each other about this. Worship and study were named by most as being of fundamental importance to them, but only a very few reported feeling fed by either. The average age of those attending worship is sixty-eight years old. We have five children and no youth.

The report went on to detail the shifts that had taken place in the community over the previous fifteen years and what community leaders had to say about the challenges faced by the community and the people who lived there, and their best guess of what the next ten years would bring. Following this assessment was a section on the financial situation of the church, noting that the congregation funded 40 percent of its budget through endowment monies. At this rate the congregation would be able to afford a full-time pastor for five more years. The task force also posited that if Lewis United continued on its current path, finances and the deaths of members would force its closing within fifteen years. The report concluded with an overview of renewal's aims, the work that faces a congregation and its leaders, and the challenges that are commonly experienced. The task force said it believed that the congregation had the resources and the will for renewal and recommended this as the path.

When a task force brings its recommendation to the governing board, its goal is to share what it has learned in such a way that the board understands the recommendation and has the information it needs to make a wise decision. The right way to do this sharing is unique to your congregation's situation. You'll want to reflect on questions like these: If you've been bringing periodic updates on your work to the board, what have you learned about how best to communicate with the board? What will board members need from you if they are really to understand what you're bringing? What is your recommendation, and what about it is important to you? How did you reach that conclusion? Your task is to help the board follow your thinking and to hear the depths of your personal convictions.

Once the governing board concurs that the congregation's current course is unacceptable and that renewal is the path to which the congregation is called, the congregation then moves into phase 2 of the renewal process—surfacing a guiding vision. As they proceed, leaders must remain firmly committed to renewal. For the congregation to move successfully through renewal, leaders must dedicate themselves to helping the congregation discern and walk a new path. Challenges will arise that stall or stop any forward movement. Some people will become satisfied with the progress already made and slip into complacency. Others, experiencing the stress and conflict that change brings, will advocate drawing back. The congregation's governing board must provide the strong, steady voice that is unwilling to settle for less than it discerns God has in mind for the congregation.

Discussion Questions

1. What "aha's" did you have as you read this chapter?

2. As you think about developing readiness for renewal, what do you imagine will be the biggest challenge for your congregation?

3. Would you better enjoy the work of the germination group or the renewal task force? Why?

4. Think about the committees and groups you've been a part of at your church. What are the norms—the "ten commandments" for how people work together and how things get done?

5. If forming the germination group were your responsibility, how would you go about it, and whom would you approach?

6. What do you think the purpose of the church is? What would you say is the difference a congregation is supposed to make in the lives of its members and in the lives of the people in the surrounding community? What is the difference that makes to the world?

7. One of the tasks of the renewal task force is learning the current reality of the congregation and the community surrounding it. What are your assumptions about what's true of your congregation? What are your assumptions about the surrounding community?

8. What's your sense of what will be true of your congregation in five years if its life and work together remain as they are now? In ten years?

9. If you think your congregation needs renewing, why do you think so? What needs to be different? What would the result of that change be?

4
Surfacing a Guiding Vision
EXPANDING THE CONGREGATION'S OPENNESS TO GOD

Phase 1 prepared the congregation's leaders to begin leading the congregation in renewal. Phase 2 extends the concept and experiences of renewal to a larger group of people within the congregation and addresses the question of vision. In small and large gatherings, people remind themselves, through conversation and the telling of stories, of the difference their faith has made and continues to make in their lives. They reflect on Scripture and on those peak moments when the congregation embodied biblical models of Christian community and service.

Then, having developed a new perspective on congregational life, they dream about shifts that renewal would bring if those peak moments were the norm. They project the difference that renewal would make for themselves and for those beyond the congregation's doors. All the while they are practicing a new way of being a community as they speak openly of their thoughts and feelings, listen with curiosity to each other and to God, and together act with intention.

The various steps of phase two lead to four outcomes, the most obvious of which is a vision of the renewed congregation capable of guiding future planning. All four outcomes, however, are necessary to prepare the congregation and its leaders for the work of phase 3, *living into the vision*. The steps in phase 2 result in:

- broadened involvement and formation of the congregation

- clarity about the congregation's mission and values

- discernment and adoption of a vision

- commitment on the part of the congregation's leaders to achieve this vision

As the congregation gets ready to chart a new course, it needs to open itself to God's leading and to develop a common picture of what the congregation is called to become. This vision orients the congregation in a new direction and gives the people a specific destination toward which to aim. This specificity helps the congregation identify the key components that make this future different from the congregation's current reality. It provides direction about which aims to pursue and how best to align human and financial resources to achieve the desired results.

The congregation's journey, like that of the Hebrew people during the Exodus, will be unpredictable and full of moments when people doubt the wisdom of embarking on this work. During times of discouragement, a clear picture and a deep desire for the congregation's "promised land" provide motivation to keep going. An ability to sense God's presence provides courage and peace in the midst of chaos.

Phase 2 is a period of spiritual formation just as much as it is a time of vision formation. Don't skip past or rush through the steps that focus on preparation of the congregation and leaders. A vision created quickly in a rush of emotion, or one that people accept with their heads but don't truly want, will lead you nowhere. Both hearts and heads must be engaged. Likewise,

---

Phase 2 addresses the spiritual formation of the people as well as the formation of a guiding vision.

---

don't skip the final step of creating an accountability structure. The world is full of congregations that created sparkling vision statements and then never did anything with them.

If you come to a step that has you thinking, "Our congregation would never do this," find a way to ease the people into it. Should you reach a step that seems to the people like something they've done in the past, find a way to help the congregation approach the work in a fresh way. Each step of this phase is important. Although you may not see direct results from attending to the work of a particular step, you will feel the impact further down the road if you neglect it.

Who Participates in Phase 2?

Phase 2 involves the entire congregation. It challenges all to deepen their understanding of the purpose and mission of the church and congregations, and to expand their openness to God and to each other. People's involvement and level of participation will vary from step to step. Some steps require work on the part of small groupings of leaders. Other steps invite the whole congregation to participate. We'll be referring to five specific groups of people in this phase of renewal work.

The Congregation's Governing Board
At the conclusion of phase 1, the congregation's governing board reached the decision that the current trajectory of the congregation was unacceptable. The board must now begin surfacing the vision that will guide a new trajectory. In phase 1, the board delegated the work of assessing the need for renewal to another group, the renewal task force. Phase 2 will need a similar guiding group, which we call the *vision team* to differentiate it from previous groups and to highlight its purpose. This team's work requires a singleness of focus and a time commitment that the governing board, with its many responsibilities, can't provide.

The governing board forms this team, gives it a clear assignment, and assesses the team's progress at regular intervals.

At the end of phase 2, the work comes back to the governing board. This group has the responsibility of charting the congregation's course and guiding it along the way. The vision needs to be formally and willingly adopted by the board, with as full as possible an awareness of what this new trajectory will demand of it and the congregation. Phase 2 concludes with the board's developing accountability structures to ensure that it and the other leaders in the congregation will design and deliver strategies that keep moving the congregation toward God's vision for it.

The Vision Team

The vision team designs and implements processes to help the congregation and its leaders open themselves to Scripture, to each other, and to God's voice, so that the people can surface the vision that will guide them toward renewal. The team should include some who served on the renewal task force in order to ensure continuity and bring the group to an intimate awareness of the work already accomplished. Those selected for this team should be people who are trusted by the congregation and who have a heart for the work involved. They must also have the expertise and skills to accomplish the tasks assigned to them. These tasks include:

- coordinating and organizing
- designing or finding appropriate processes for group gatherings
- leading group gatherings in a way that fosters Christian community
- synthesizing information
- communicating regularly with the governing board and congregation

This phase addresses building up neglected or never-formed faith muscles in the congregation's members.

The Congregation as a Whole

Congregational renewal increases a congregation's ability to notice and experience God in its midst. It strengthens a congregation's desire to partner with God in achieving God's aims for the world, and enhances its ability to be the body of Christ in the world for the sake of the world. Phase 2 provides the opportunity for the entire congregation to build up neglected or never-formed faith muscles and invites members to join the leaders in thinking missionally and exploring the "why" of its existence. People reflect on who they are as a congregation. They explore what the congregation has historically valued and the congregation's role in the community across the years. They reflect on what was going on in those moments when the congregation embodied the best of what church can be.

From that place of discovery, the congregation participates in discerning the new future to which God is calling it. The percentage of a congregation actively involved in the vision process depends, to some extent, on the size of the congregation. Generally, the smaller the congregation, the greater the percentage of people who actively participate in surfacing the vision.

Current and Future Leaders

Any interested person in the congregation should be given the opportunity to participate in the discernment and envisioning activities. Strategies, however, must be developed to ensure that current leaders are active participants in the process. These people are the backbone of the current congregation. Their participation will influence their leadership of the congregation even as the vision emerges.

The development of the congregation depends not only on the current leaders, but also on those who over time will step into leadership roles. For the congregation to live into the future envisioned, both current and future leaders must have a connection and commitment to the vision. Without making assumptions about future roles of individuals, the vision team develops a list of people whom they believe should participate in the discernment process. The team looks especially for individuals who seem to embody the congregation's future and who bring a fresh perspective. In addition to any general invitation given to the congregation, the team develops strategies to encourage these individuals to participate.

The Pastor and Ministry Staff

As spiritual leaders of the congregation, pastors often initiate renewal and can be among the first to sense God's longings for the people. Throughout the renewal process these spiritual leaders continue to sense God's leading and to form opinions about God's desires. Good leadership dictates that they also equip others to do this work. While maintaining a prophetic role, wise pastors know that God speaks through many voices. They encourage the congregation to listen for and discern God's vision, even knowing that it may be different from what the pastor had originally foreseen.

The vision finally adopted must be owned, embraced, and acted upon by the people. Pastors come and go, while the congregation and God's vision remain. While serving in this place, pastors are charged with overseeing the development of both individuals and the congregation, helping them discern and live into God's purposes for them. Knowing they have responsibility for the overall health of the congregation, pastors exercise not only spiritual leadership but also organizational leadership. From their unique perspective, pastors help lay leaders reflect on how individual activities and processes can work together to ensure the development of both the people and the congregation. To carry out their role, pastors must be integrally involved in the process. We recommend that they be active members of key leadership teams, including the vision team.

We recommend that any ministry staff members participate actively along with the congregation in the work of phase 2. They do this for their own continual personal formation, for the sake of the insights they bring, and as a way of modeling involvement for others. The ministry team, with the leadership of the pastor, must model for the congregation the openness to God and each other that will be asked of all members.

The Steps of Phase 2

The work of phase 2 involves nine steps. These steps fall into three stages of work. Steps 1 and 2 focus on organizing and planning for the work ahead. Steps 3 through 7 involve deepening the congregation's relationship with God and surfacing a vision. The final stage of work, steps 8 and 9, addresses the development of commitment and follow-through.

These steps are the activities of the externally focused work of this phase. Addressing each one in order will further renewal, *but only* if each is addressed in a way that helps people attend to the internal work of deepening their skills of "being community" and collectively listening to God. The external work of this phase is straightforward, surfacing a vision. The internal work demanded of the people is more complex. You can't receive a new vision unless you're willing to give up the one you hold. In phase 2, the people ground themselves in God's love and intent for them and for the world. Anchored in that reality, they let go of their preconceived notions of the congregation and open themselves to let their opinions and perspectives be shaped by God. For a time they live in the uncomfortable space of not knowing. They don't know where they're heading or how they'll get there. Rather than turning to their own

Surfacing a guiding vision requires people to let go of their picture of the future and learn to dream God's dream for their congregation.

wisdom to sort out this uncertainty, they turn to God. They listen together until they have a strong sense of God's leading and a picture of the difference God wants to make in the world through their particular congregation.

The congregation shifts as the people who make up the congregation experience internal shifts in attitude and behavior. These shifts take place as people:

- name the current reality
- ground themselves in God
- let go of preconceived ideas about the congregation and its future
- open themselves to God for direction
- sense God's leading
- choose a path

As you work through each step, you'll need to keep both the named task and this inner work in mind. Balancing this duality is part of what makes renewal difficult. Congregations tend to address one or the other when both are needed. Working through the steps keeps the process moving. Nurturing the internal transition of the people fosters the transformation.

Step 1: The Governing Board Appoints the Vision Team

The congregation's governing board initiates phase 2 when it selects and authorizes a vision team. The governing board needs to be clear about the task it is asking this group of people to undertake and the results the board is asking the team to achieve. The board should be able to describe as well where the vision team's authority starts and stops. Clarity about the task's boundaries and goals helps the board select the right people for the team and then orient them to their work. Prospective team members need to understand the task before they can determine whether they can say yes to this sizable job.

The vision team should represent the diversity within the congregation; it should be composed of people who inspire trust. Keep in mind that this group will be given a specific task to accomplish. The members must design strategies and persuade people to participate. They must be task-oriented enough to get things done in timely ways. They must be able to help others understand and address this required inner work. And like the rest of the congregation, team members must be able and willing to set aside their own pictures of the congregation's best future for the sake of hearing God's ideas.

The team must surface a vision of the renewed congregation and do it in a way that involves all of the current leaders of the congregation and as much of the congregation as possible. The governing board should specify a time frame for the work, including due dates for progress reports to the board throughout the process. We recommend that the board ask the team to develop an overarching plan and a more detailed time line for its work before proceeding. This plan would be reviewed and approved by the board before implementation.

Step 2: The Vision Team Establishes Itself
The vision team's first order of business is to establish itself as a team—not a collection of individuals, but one body with a

---

The vision team does not surface the vision itself, but involves leaders and as much of the congregation as possible in this work.

Team members must develop a common understanding of both their task and the way they want to work together.

---

common aim. Before tackling their work, team members need to reach a common understanding of the task before them and the expected outcomes. This step aligns the team members' thinking and focuses their energy in the same direction. Team members often arrive at their first meeting with very different ideas about what they've been asked to do.

The team should go over the assignment given by the board and the steps outlined in this chapter. If there are discrepancies between what the decision-making body has authorized and what the team senses is needed to do its work, it must negotiate the terms of its assignment with the board. The board and team must function as partners, working together to achieve a common aim.

It's helpful for the team members to share with each other why they said yes to the task. Each agreed for a slightly different reason. Each has some kind of personal investment in the project or outcome. Knowing what those reasons are up front will help the team members understand each other's motivations and work together more effectively as a unified body.

Once clear about the task, the team members establish agreements about how they want to work together. This covenanting puts the responsibility for creating satisfying and effective working relationships on the members themselves. How shall we work together, specifically? What are our expectations about attendance at meetings? What's our policy about sharing information with people not on our team? How do we want to deal with conflict or disagreements? What kind of spirit and atmosphere do we want to prevail at our meetings? And what do we need to do to help ensure that?

Developing team agreements helps the members know what they can count on from each other. The agreements are helpful only to the extent that the people building them are honest with each other about their needs and preferences. It helps no one to build agreements that sound nice but that no one really intends to keep. The team at First Church created a great list of team agreements, and then went on to violate virtually all of them on a regular basis. By the time the team called us, frustration had grown so high that the work had stalled completely, and two team members had stopped attending worship.

Identify the key things you need from each other, and don't make agreements that you know you can't or don't intend to deliver on. We encourage teams to keep visible at each meeting both their team agreements and a statement summarizing their task. This structure reminds team members why they're there and how they've agreed to work together. Having the agreements and task visible invites team members to use the team's own words to call it back on course when it strays.

In addition to developing a common understanding of the task and how team members will work together, the team needs to find ways to keep itself open to the influence of God's spirit. A team can know exactly what it's doing and precisely how to work together and yet leave God totally out of the picture. For the team to work creatively and to embody the openness to God it is working to foster in the congregation, the team must find ways to stay open to God. Discussing what team members believe to be God's hopes for their work can be a helpful way to begin. Right from the start, the team mindfully aligns its efforts with God's interests. Team agreements should be modified as necessary so that they reflect the group's best sense of God's will. The team needs to feel God as a real presence on the team if the group is to embody Christian community.

Embodying Christian community, while certainly providing a more fulfilling experience for team members, sets the tone for the rest of the congregation. We once heard church consultant Roy Oswald say that a congregation will grow no deeper spiritually than the people at its core. We have found

The team does not operate alone; it must find ways to stay connected and open to God.

that statement to be true. The people cannot go where the leaders will not lead. For the congregation to step into new and generative ways of speaking and listening to one another and to God, the vision team must be willing to go there first.

Teams that find themselves stuck or frustrated often find it helpful to revisit their understanding of the task, their team agreements, and their level of openness to God's Spirit. What is the larger goal our efforts are trying to serve? What's most important to the congregation about this issue we're wrestling with? What's important to God about it? What's most important for us to keep in mind right now? Is there something about the way we're working together that is getting in our way? What do we each sense God's word might be to us to be right now?

Step 3: The Vision Team Develops a Plan
Once the team is clear about its assignment and has established how it will work together while remaining open to God, it moves on to developing an overall plan. The plan encompasses the next four steps of phase 2:

- deepening the congregation's openness to God
- surfacing the vision
- refining the vision
- testing and further refining the vision

This chapter specifies what the work of each of those steps entails, who's involved, and what each step must accomplish. The appendixes provide tools and suggest other resources that may be helpful as you plan the best way for your congregation to move through each step. You will not find in the back of this book however, a detailed plan to follow.

While some resources on congregational renewal tell you precisely how and when to do the work, we do not find that such specific instructions ultimately serve a congregation's best interests. Each congregation is unique, and the strategies and timing that work best differ greatly. Feel free to incorporate processes others have found helpful, but don't simply replicate another congregation's exact plan and expect to get the same results.

Though no one plan fits every congregation, a particular sequencing of steps helps a congregation achieve renewal. Certain work must be done at certain points in the process, and specific perspectives and skills must be developed. Successful renewal efforts follow the path we describe in this book. What differs among congregations that have been successful is what they did to move through each step and how long they took to do it. A step that is taken quickly in one congregation may take many months in another. Let your knowledge of your congregation guide you as you reflect on each step. "What will be the best way for us to do that here? Realistically, how long will it likely take us to accomplish this step, so that the work is done well and prepares us for what comes next?"

An effective method of planning is for the team first to name the desired outcome for each of the next four steps of phase 2, and then to identify the current reality of the congregation in relation to each outcome. The vision team at St. John's named one of the desired outcomes for step 4 as *the congregation must want to hear and follow God's wisdom about the congregation's future*. It then reflected on how the congregation made decisions about its future and made the following observations:

- Committees and teams do not overtly seek God's wisdom in their decision making.

- In the past, all-church meetings have asked for people's opinions, rather than for their sense of God's opinion.

- Congregational prayers during worship tend to be for people, community groups, and world affairs. Rarely does anyone pray for the congregation.

- Our congregation has very little recent experience in listening for God's opinion about the congregation.

Clear about both the desired outcome and the starting place, the vision team designed strategies to help move the congregation from where it was to a new reality. Once the strategies had been identified, the team developed an estimated time line for the work. As you can see, developing a plan takes a good deal of energy and thought. Chapter 6 talks more about planning and provides a planning process you may wish to use to help you develop your plan.

The vision team's plan for each step provides both a guide for its work and a way to communicate clearly with the board and the congregation about its intentions. The plan keeps the team focused and moving in a timely fashion. It also names points in the process for evaluating the effects of the team's actions. If your experience is typical, you will find that your well-crafted plan will need to be adjusted along the way. New insights about the congregation, unexpected happenings, a component that moves faster or slower than anticipated—all can affect the plan. Expect the unexpected. Include in your time line points at which you'll stop and ask such questions as these: Are we getting the results we wanted? If not, what might we need to shift? What do we know now that we didn't know before, and how does that knowledge affect what we've planned?

You may choose to build detailed plans that guide the entirety of phase 2. If this is the case, note places to assess how things

---

The team's plan keeps it focused and provides a way to monitor progress.

---

are going so that you can adjust your plans accordingly. Or you may decide to plan as you go along, using what you learn in step 4 to build a plan for step 5, and so on. If this is more your style, be sure to set dates when that planning will take place. The best time to plan your next step is before you finish taking your current one.

Plan, too, to communicate. Congregations become anxious when they are not kept informed about what's going to happen next. Anxiety seems to rise particularly with the surfacing, refinement, and adoption of the vision. We find that often the vision team and other leaders are so immersed in the work that they assume everyone knows what they know. "Surely one or two announcements and an article in the newsletter will suffice to let folks know what's going on." You cannot communicate too much. Convey your plans. Be open with information. Speak. Write. Post reports. Send letters. Ask for questions and answer them. Anxious people are resistant people, and the members of the congregation need to be open—open to God and open to one another.

Step 4: The Congregation Deepens its Openness to God and Anchors Itself in God's Aims

Christian discernment is a practice used by congregations to align their lives and ministries more fully with God's purposes and aims. In discerning a guiding vision, a congregation seeks to discover what God desires the congregation to be and do in this place and time. The practice of discernment is based on certain principles. Four seem of prime importance.

1. God is actively at work in the world.

2. God is greater and wiser than the congregation.

3. God wants something both for the congregation and for the people served by the congregation.

4. God will communicate those desires if the congregation will listen.

The congregation needs to reach the point of believing that God has an opinion about the congregation's future that is more insightful than its own.

For discernment to reflect a congregation's best sense of God's desires, rather than a glorification of personal whims and wants, the congregation must be anchored in an understanding of who God is and what God is about in the world. The congregation must believe that God has an opinion about the congregation's future that is more insightful than its own. And it must truly want to hear and follow that wisdom. If a congregation does not enter discernment with these attitudes largely in place, the exercise is futile.

This is not brand-new work. Those who were active participants in phase 1 did some of this anchoring work. Now it's time for the congregation at large to reflect on its work and the world from God's perspective. "How is God active in the world today? What difference does God envision the church making in the world? What role does God see individual faith communities playing? What is the purpose of *our* congregation in God's eyes? What difference are we supposed to be making in our own and others' lives? What is our mission?"

We call this *missional thinking*. It directs the mind and heart to reflect on the primary mission of a congregation from God's perspective, allowing the congregation to then plan and act from that sense. The overarching aim of congregational renewal is the development of a missional mind-set and heart-set that guides all aspects of a congregation's life. This step of phase 2 invites the congregation to begin exploring these waters without asking that the people, at this point, make any decisions or take any actions. Later in phase 2, the congregation will make decisions about its future. Phase 3 will require people to act on those decisions, making real shifts in how the congregation lives and works together. In preparation, the congregation needs time to think about, explore, and accept the basic underlying premises—that God has a mission for the congregation and that the congregation's job is to discover it and do it.

Strive to involve as much of the congregation as possible, and be aware that people may not be eager to take part in what you have so carefully planned. Some in the congregation may have had experiences with renewal efforts that left them jaded and less than eager to participate. Others are busy, and happy to leave the work to others. You will need to be creative.

As possible, use the groupings and gatherings that are already in place. The team at St. Brendan's knew that getting people to come out another evening or afternoon of the week would be fruitless. As much as possible, they used short bits of time in existing group gatherings to run their processes. Taking this time was done, of course, with the agreement of those leading the groups. For seven months, the choir, the finance committee, the women's circle, the youth group, the staff—all the groups and teams—set aside the first twenty minutes of their meetings to engage in dialogue around questions designed to help them converse about their experiences of God and God's aims for congregations. Additional gatherings were held after worship, in homes, and even in retirement centers for members who weren't part of an ongoing group but who wanted to take part.

Worship offers the opportunity to touch the broadest group of people and to deepen their thinking. Liturgy and preaching in phase 2 should root people in God's aims for people and the world. Examining God's call and the response of other faithful individuals and communities throughout history can help the congregation begin to wonder about God's present call to the congregation.

Educational settings within the congregation offer other arenas for inviting people into missional thinking. Short-term classes or home study groups might be offered to give people an opportunity to reflect more deeply on the purpose of church and the nature of God's callings. Give as many people

---

Don't move on to surfacing a vision until people are ready not only to dream God's dream, but to act on it.

---

as possible opportunities to study together and talk with each other about God's call to individuals and faith communities throughout history. This reflection helps prepare them to discern God's movement in their midst now.

How long does this step take? We recommend holding off on beginning vision events until the congregation has had at least several months of this kind of preparation, perhaps even a year. You're looking to build in people the desire to dream and the willingness to turn to God as the giver of that dream. Take your time. Efforts invested now will pay dividends later. Those intimately involved in the workings of the congregation may feel that they are prepared after a few weeks. To get a sense of pacing, look to more average congregants. What's the mood during the coffee hour after worship? When conversations beyond Sunday morning turn to church, what do people talk about? Is there a sense of eagerness? A deepened expression of Christian community? Can people have thoughtful and well-grounded conversations with others about the future of the congregation, trying to see it from God's perspective as well as their own? If not, what seems to be needed, and how might you help meet that need? Do not move on to trying to surface a vision until you sense that people are expressing a readiness to dream God's dream—and then to live into it.

Step 5: Surfacing the Vision

Up to now, the work has been preparing the leaders and people of the congregation to receive the dream of a new future. Now the work takes a turn. It's time to ask: What *is* the future God is calling our congregation to? What does God want to do through us? *Surfacing* the vision implies that a vision for your congregation already exists. We believe that such a vision *does* exist. When a congregation tunes itself to the heart of the God, it can hear what God has in mind.

This step will take some time. Your goal is to involve as many as possible in discerning God's vision for the congregation. A vision is a picture of what the congregation would be doing, how the members would feel about it, and what impact it would have beyond the church doors if the congregation lived out its mission in the fullest way possible. The congregation's mission may be timeless, but its vision reflects the current gifts and needs of the congregation, community, and world. St. Luke's understands its mission to be the same today as it was sixty years ago: "making Christian disciples who share God's love and hope." In 1968, living out that mission meant bringing into discipleship the young Anglo families moving into its rapidly growing community. In 2008, it means working with retirees of multiple ethnicities who are now the primary residents in the area around the church. Discerning a new vision requires letting go of old ones.

Letting go of an old vision is particularly difficult for the people who were involved in its formation. Many of those "young Anglo families," now no longer young, are still active members at St. Luke's. Their picture of a renewed St. Luke's had always included significant ministry to families and children. With fewer and fewer young families in the area, this was not likely to be God's vision for the congregation. Letting go of that dream was painful and evoked feelings of failure. Be aware that this step will involve the death of some people's dreams, and that's never easy or painless.

Surfacing the vision needs to be done by a broad base of the congregation. It is rare for any one person to be granted the vision in its totality. The vision will be more fully developed and widely embraced when it has been surfaced through processes that encourage people to dream separately and in accord across a span of time. The vision and its various components will direct

Use vision processes that give people ample time to think, speak, listen, and pray together.

your congregation's efforts and allocation of resources across the next several years. Do not rush its development. This is a task for the heart and the spirit, as well as the mind. Choose or develop processes that give people time to think, to speak, to listen, and to pray. Help people be open and curious with each other and with God.

A myriad of resources offer processes for discerning a congregation's guiding vision. Appendix B lists some approaches you may wish to consider using. Many others exist. We find vision processes based on the principles of Appreciative Inquiry or Asset Mapping particularly well suited to congregations. Both encourage a positive attitude and generative relationships. Each helps groups reframe their story and see themselves as people with the power to make choices. (Two helpful books are listed in the resource section.) The process that will work best for your congregation is the one that best matches the congregation's faith language, preferred working style, and situation. Elements we've found to be important include:

- significant anchoring in biblical material
- processes for identifying the congregation's mission and its values
- processes for identifying the strengths, challenges, needs, and opportunities of the congregation and community
- space and time for people to explore freely and imagine possibilities
- ways for listening to God as a community
- opportunities for deep and honest conversations with others

- feedback loops that keep participants informed and participating as the vision develops
- a skilled facilitator

Provide people with a variety of settings for reflecting and talking with each other. Small-group settings give each person more time to talk. They encourage deeper sharing and more probing explorations of material. Large-group settings offer people the opportunity to hear more perspectives and to get a sense of the broader thinking emerging within the congregation. Should there be sensitive information to share or teaching to be done on a complex subject, a large-group setting ensures that everyone hears the same thing at the same time. Know what you're trying to achieve when you gather people together, and use settings of various sizes to help you accomplish your objectives.

Surfacing God's vision through group discernment should continue to form the people participating just as surely as it forms a vision. Those participating come away from such processes more open to God and more able to listen. Discernment engages both head and heart. People think and speak. They feel and respond. They talk and listen. They wait. Discernment asks a group to set aside preconceived ideas and personal agendas. Discernment seeks God's ideas and God's agenda.

The specific, identifiable result of this step is a vision, a picture of the future congregation that the current congregation believes God is calling it to become. We recommend that your vision take the form of either a narrative paragraph or a list of components that describe the congregation in concrete terms. This vision should be specific to your current time and situation. We've found that while pithy one-sentence visions are

---

Surfacing the vision should be a time of spiritual and faith formation for participants.

The vision should be specific enough to guide planning. It should excite and energize people.

---

memorable, they don't provide much guidance for setting specific goals. You'll be using this vision to guide planning. The form you choose must be able to serve that purpose. Sometimes this statement is roughly drafted by the gathered group and put on paper by the person facilitating the process. Sometimes the vision team creates the draft to summarize the work of the larger group. However it's done, the words need to find their way onto paper.

Participants generally want the vision to be complete at this point and are frustrated that it is not. Be assured that it is normal at this stage for the vision to be unfinished. There's more work to be done. A smaller group can do this refining work more easily, and so the vision is passed on to the vision team.

Step 6: Refining the Vision

The vision passed to the vision team may need very little work. Or it may require extensive fleshing out or paring down. In whatever shape the vision arrives, it's the vision team's job now to make sure that the vision adequately captures what surfaced in discernment and that it is complete enough to guide the congregation's planning. Whether the vision is a three-to-five-year proposal or one that may take a decade or more to complete is far less important than whether it can guide planning.

Does the vision represent a strongly held consensus of understanding, or does it reflect the thinking of only one or two people? Are there elements that we sense are missing? Is the vision specific enough to guide our planning? Would someone who hadn't participated in the vision process understand what these words and phrases mean? Is there a clearer way to express what has been said? Does this vision serve the congregation's mission? Does it express the congregation's values? Does this vision call us to something bigger? Does it excite and energize us? Does it feel like it's of God?

The vision team works on behalf of the congregation, its leaders, and God. Its primary task here is to make sure that the vision is functional. After refinement, the vision will be given back to the congregation to ensure that it is an accurate reflection of the members' sense of God's call.

Here is the vision that resulted from one congregation's discernment:

We will be a diverse community that:

- shares our faith

- nurtures people of all ages in discipleship

- worships in a variety of ways and enjoys a vibrant music ministry

- moves us beyond our comfort zones to extend God's love

Initially, the vision team believed that the vision was complete and needed no additional refinement. The vision seemed clear and appeared to be an accurate summation of the group's work. But as it thought about using the statement as a basis for planning, the team realized that an important element was missing. While particular ministry areas were identified as key to the congregation's future, the difference to be made by those ministries was missing. As one person noted about the area of music ministry, "A vibrant music ministry can achieve many things. What's our primary purpose in having one? To entertain? To inspire? What? Unless we're specific, the vision won't provide us with the direction we need it to."

The team looked at the first statement, "shares our faith," and asked, "What purpose is this action supposed to serve? What intent did we hear in those vision sessions?" "How could this aim be said more clearly and in a way that inspires us to do it?" Team members referred to the notes they had made during the gatherings and sharpened the statement. The team reviewed each of the statements in this way. It tried to make each statement convey a fuller sense of what it heard the congregation say. It worked to make each statement precise, so that as groups used the statements to guide their planning, each one would provide an accurate compass. The refined version of the vision read:

We will be a faith community where:

- people easily and naturally introduce others to Jesus Christ

- children, youth, and adults have a life-giving and growing relationship with Jesus Christ that guides their life

- worship connects people with their deepest selves and with God

- music expresses our understanding and experience of God and is an avenue for spiritual growth

- people regularly move beyond their comfort zones and the doors of the church to share God's love and to serve the needs of the community and the world

The team members then prepared a written report for the governing board. They presented the refined vision—not as a final product, but as a draft. Thinking about their work as simply another draft of the vision was difficult for some members of the team. After working so diligently, they'd become quite attached to the vision as it now stood.

We strongly recommend that you include not just your refined statement of the vision, but also the supporting material that came out of the work that led to your reshaping of the vision. Your report should help people understand why shifts

If the congregation doesn't truly want the future the vision represents, renewal will progress no further.

have been made and the purpose they serve. This approach puts information in people's hands and helps prevent misunderstandings. The report's goal is both to document the work and to equip the board and the congregation to refine the vision even further.

Step 7: Testing and Further Refinement

In the renewal process, a congregation faces multiple challenges. One challenge often surfaces once the governing board has seen and responded favorably to the initial refining of the vision. The board has in its hands a vision that emerged from the work of the people, one refined enough to guide planning. The tendency is to rejoice and declare the vision process complete. However, the fact that the congregation participated and that something has been put on paper does not mean that the congregation truly owns the vision. Nor does it mean that the vision is complete.

For the congregation to continue to move forward toward renewal, the vision must be written not only on paper, but also in the hearts of people. In Jeremiah God says, "This is the covenant I will make with the house of Israel after that time. . . . I will put my law in their minds and write it on their hearts. I will be their God, and they will be my people" (31:33). The objective in the refining and testing step is to make sure the vision is written on the people's hearts as well as in their minds. The vision may sound inspiring and make sense, but if a majority of the congregation doesn't want it and isn't willing to "go there," very little will happen.

People must be given the opportunity to step back from their initial envisioning work and reflect on what they have surfaced.

They have the opportunity now to reflect on, pray about, test out, and adjust the vision. "Is this really what God wants? Is it really what we want? How does it need to be shifted to express more accurately God's future to which we commit ourselves?" For the vision to have the power to sustain the people in their work, it must accurately express what they deeply desire for themselves and their congregation. The guiding vision will be used to steer the church, and it will mean change. No fooling! That reality must sink in. The congregation may not fully understand the implications of adopting the vision, if past envisioning work has had no effect.

The congregation reflects on questions like these: How does this vision embody what we sense is truly important to God? How does it embody what is truly important to me and to us? How does it need to be adjusted to express more accurately what is important? What will be the implications for me and for the congregation as we begin to live into this future? If we say yes to this vision, to what will we be saying no? How much do we actually want this future for our congregation? Are we willing to do what it takes to get there?

The settings for this work vary from congregation to congregation, depending somewhat on the congregation's size. One of the easiest and most helpful strategies is to plan for these testing-the-vision gatherings at the same time you plan for discernment gatherings, framing the second set of events as follow-up sessions. This step ties the work together in the congregation's mind, puts dates on people's calendars, and keeps the process flowing.

After the congregation has had a chance to review and offer suggestions or refinements to the vision, the vision team again synthesizes the input from the people and takes this revision to the board. This back-and-forth work between the vision team and the congregation continues for as long as it takes to form a vision that "sings" for the people, until it feels compelling, right, and full. When this point is reached, the task of the vision team is complete.

When the governing board adopts the vision, it commits to using the congregation's human and fiscal resources to achieve specific results.

Step 8: Counting the Cost and Officially Adopting the Vision

The governing board now has a vision surfaced and owned by the people. In a small church the total congregation may officially adopt the vision. In a larger church, formal adoption may be an action of the governing board. Whichever the board decides is best, this step has far-reaching significance. By formally adopting the vision, the congregation (or the board on behalf of the congregation) commits to aligning the congregation's fiscal and human resources to achieve a specific set of results. The body must pause before taking this action and seriously ask itself one last time, "Do we really want to do this?"

In the Gospel of Luke, Jesus reminds the large crowd following him of the ramifications of committing to a life as his disciple. Choosing that path comes with costs: "Suppose one of you wants to build a tower. Will he not first sit down and estimate the cost to see if he has enough money to complete it?" (Luke 14:28). Before committing to lead the congregation steadfastly in this new direction, the voting body needs to count the cost and makes sure of its commitment to proceed.

Of course, it's impossible to know the full cost of renewal ahead of time. However, we urge the board or congregation to stop again and imagine the implications of living into the vision. "What are we now doing that we will have to stop doing? What do we now do that, while it may continue, will receive no further assistance? Who will be most affected? Who will feel the loss most strongly? Who will call for a return to functioning as we have in the past? Do we believe this is the right way to proceed even if doing so results in currently active members' choosing to become less active? Even if it means some will leave the congregation?"

Creating an accountability structure helps the governing board follow through on its intentions.

As changes begin to be made in phase 3, resistance will emerge. Certainly not all the resistance points can be anticipated. Simply naming some of the challenges that might arise helps leaders begin to develop the ability and commitment to work with resistance and to resolve not to be co-opted by pressure to return to the old path.

Once the board or congregation determines that it will follow the call of the vision, it formally adopts the vision. Take this action with an awareness and appreciation of what the congregation has done to reach this point, and savor the significance of the moment. This is an act of faithfulness on the part of the congregation and an act of commitment by leaders to do all that is necessary for the congregation to act faithfully.

Step 9: Developing an Accountability Structure

Your congregation has surfaced a clear vision of the future you believe God is calling you into. You've committed yourselves to do what it takes to go there. But, unless you take one more specific step, all of your work will have been in vain.

We've seen countless congregations devoutly declare their commitment and then fail to hold themselves accountable for acting on it. You've got great intentions. Now take one more step and put a structure in place that will ensure that you regularly assess the congregation's progress toward the new vision. This is called an *accountability structure* because it holds you accountable for what you've said you want to achieve.

Many if not most people resist accountability, but in renewal it's easy to slip back into old patterns without even noticing. An accountability structure continually calls you to notice whether you're living as you declare you want to live. If you find that your actions don't match your declared vision, you have two choices. Either you change your actions, or you change your vision to reflect what you truly want.

Your governing board's job now is to develop ways to hold itself accountable to what it and the congregation have said they want. No one accountability structure works better than others. We've found that people are more likely to use accountability systems they've had a hand in designing. Whatever is developed must pose certain fundamental questions to the governing board at regular intervals until the vision is achieved:

- What progress have we made toward renewal?

- What are we doing to continue the movement forward?

- Is it working? If not, what needs to be adjusted?

- What needs to happen next, and what's needed from us or other leaders for that to happen?

The Challenge of Phase 2

The challenge of phase 2 is supporting the inner transition of the people while attending to the external steps necessary for surfacing a vision. With one hand, the vision team encourages spiritual awakening and formation. With the other, it plans and organizes activities and events. Teams tend to get absorbed in the external activities, dropping the focus on the inner work. This seems especially to be true for congregations that, until now, have not focused on developing the inner life. These congregations are good at planning and running activities, and so vision team members have well-developed "muscles" in that area. It's easy and natural to default to your strong side when you grow tired, the work grows challenging, or time constraints arise.

Dialogue is one of the most powerful tools you can use to foster internal shifts. Learn how to have and facilitate conversations in which people are open with their thoughts and open to hearing the thoughts of others. Practice and learn to encourage *deep democracy* in the groups you lead. "Deep democracy"—a conversation and conflict-resolution methodology—holds that every voice in the group offers something of value to the group and that every voice within a person offers insight to that person. This attitude helps you listen with greater openness and curiosity as you look for the wisdom and the word of God within the person.

The topic you ask people to talk about and the way you phrase your questions determine the quality and depth of the conversation. When people are asked to talk about subjects that matter to them, they engage more readily, and the resulting conversation is more energized. Yes and no questions don't lend themselves to holy conversation. Don't ask questions to which you already know the answer. Learn to ask "powerful" questions, questions that help people to dig into their thoughts and feelings and to articulate their values. Powerful questions open the door to dialogue and discovery. The insights they generate provoke change within individuals and the group. Appendix C gives you examples of powerful questions and suggestions for how to have powerful conversations.

Expect phase 2 to take time. In our experience, nine months to a year is not unusual. Renewal is a process, not a race. Forcing people to make decisions they're not ready to make provokes resistance. At the same time, if the congregation doesn't sense that progress is being made, it will grow bored and dismiss renewal as just another nice idea. Be gentle with yourselves and compassionate with the congregation, but stay focused and keep moving. Remember, you are not alone on this journey. The God who called you to it is right there with you.

Discussion Questions

1. Recall a moment when you experienced your current congregation really "being church." How would the congregation be different if that were the norm?

2. What do you see as the fundamental purpose of church? What difference is a congregation supposed to make in the lives of its members and in its surrounding community?

3. What scriptures are foundational to your understanding of what a congregation is supposed to be and do?

4. What's your picture of the better future for your congregation? On a scale of one to ten, with one being low and ten being high, how able and willing are you to let go of that picture to hear God's ideas? What would help you feel more able and willing?

5. What do you sense will be needed by your congregation to help people dream God's dream for it?

5

Living into the Vision

ALIGNING THE WORK OF THE CONGREGATION WITH THE VISION

Congratulations! Having moved through phases 1 and 2, your congregation now has a new future to aim toward, desire in the hearts of people to get there, and commitment on the part of leaders to provide the leadership required to make it happen. Now what?

The Book of Proverbs reminds us that without a vision people perish (29:18, KJV). It's also true that unless strategies are developed and acted upon, very little will change. In phase 2 you dreamed together, allowing God to give you a vision of the difference your congregation could make for one another and for people you've never even met. You've accomplished a lot, and it didn't happen by accident. You planned and adjusted and kept your eye on the ultimate goal. Now it's time to apply those same skills to transforming that dream into reality. Remember that you are working for particular outcomes in both the ministries carried out by the congregation and the inner life of the congregation and its members. Renewal reorients all aspects of a congregation and its life. It develops new habits of heart and mind, establishes new relational patterns, and aligns resources and actions to support the congregation's new vision.

It's an enormous task; you can't do it all at once. Don't even try. This phase involves taking small, steady, strategic steps over the course of many years. And what's a "strategic" step? One

It's normal for people to have mixed feelings as the congregation begins phase 3 of renewal.

that is achievable, that serves the accomplishment of your vision, and that prepares the congregation to take other steps in that direction. A strategic step paves the way for further work.

At the end of phase 2, members of a congregation typically feel more appreciative of each other and more aware of God's presence than before. And yet, while the congregation desires its newly discerned future, we often find people expressing mixed feelings when it comes time to act on what the congregation said it wanted. This hesitation is normal.

Some people feel pleased and satisfied with the change they already sense in the congregation. Their experience of church has been enhanced, and they'd be happy for life to stay just as it is, for nothing further to change. In their minds, all the work's been done; now things can get back to normal. Other people will be eager to roll up their sleeves and to begin making big, sweeping changes. They're energized by the work that's been done and want to get going *now*. Some are cynical. They've been through enough renewal attempts to believe that nothing's really going to change. Still others will be worried about the direction the congregation is headed. They wonder what will happen to the congregation if it can't pull this effort off. And there are likely a few who are not pleased with the decision at all, who are thinking it's time to start looking for a new church.

On top of that ambivalence, congregational leaders are often tired at this point. The experience of the governing board of St. Timothy's Church is typical. The board ratified a new congregational vision in May, after nine months of focused work. Pleased with the outcome but tired from its efforts, the board chose to wait until September to begin addressing phase 3. When September rolled around, the vision felt further away and much less achievable. More pressing matters, like the newly leaking roof, demanded action now. In the absence of direction about how the new vision should affect their work, committees had continued with their typical fall planning. In four short months, the congregation had settled back into its preferred way of operating. It wasn't until the following May that the board began developing strategies for moving the congregation toward its vision. By that time, so much momentum had been lost that the board spent a weekend in retreat. There, it re-anchored itself in the work that had been done the previous year and noted the changes that had taken place in the neighborhood and the world during that span of time. Unfortunately, the board lost a good deal of credibility with those who had been eagerly awaiting changes.

We cannot stress strongly enough the importance of beginning phase 3 in a timely way. If you take too long a break at this point, past patterns will take over without your even being aware it is happening. These early steps don't need to be huge. You can still catch your breath. Small, strategic steps are what is needed right now. This chapter and the next will help you think through and prepare for the work of phase 3, designing and implementing strategies that align the various aspects of the congregation toward the vision. This chapter will:

- guide you in forming a "balcony team" to manage this phase of renewal
- identify and explore the six focuses of the work
- alert you to the unique challenges of this phase

The Balcony Team

The first task of phase 3 is for the governing board to determine who will manage this final but long phase of renewal. Individuals and committees will continue designing and implementing

---

The congregation needs an officially sanctioned group to shepherd it through the remaining work of renewal.

---

the congregation's ministries and support tasks. But some group has to be charged with seeing that the work results in particular outcomes and that those outcomes move the congregation toward its vision. The pastor alone cannot carry that responsibility. Nor, in our opinion, can the existing governing board. While that body does have final responsibility and maintains ultimate oversight of the renewal process, its other duties require its full attention. Phase 3 proceeds most smoothly when a small group or team is charged with the specific responsibility of shepherding the congregation through the remainder of renewal.

Congregations take different approaches in forming this group. We encourage you to assign your team a name appropriate for your particular congregation. As a way of emphasizing its role of overseeing the movement of renewal through the congregational systems, we will call this group the *balcony team*. Ron Heifitz, senior lecturer on public leadership at Harvard's Kennedy School, likens one aspect of leadership to going up to a balcony at a dance. If you spend the entire evening on the dance floor, you're aware of only what happens in your immediate vicinity. You focus your energy on dancing—and on not colliding with the people next to you. At the end of an evening you might come home thinking, "What a great dance! Tons of people, wonderful music." If you'd gone up to the balcony, however, you would have seen something different. All the people were clustered at the far end of the hall away from the band, many sat on the sidelines, and most danced only when the music was fast. By viewing the proceedings from the balcony and broadening your perspective, you'd come away with a very different assessment of how the evening went (*Leadership on the Line*, Harvard Business School Press, 2002).

In a congregation, a balcony team:

- keeps a big-picture view of the congregation and its journey through renewal

- helps the congregation's leaders continually reflect on how their areas of congregational life can contribute to the congregation's achieving its vision

- encourages and supports leaders in making needed changes

- monitors the congregational "temperature," keeping the board apprised of the impact of renewal efforts on the congregation

This team spends much of its time up in the balcony, assessing progress from a broad perspective. Team members observe the congregation and the impact of renewal as movement is made toward the vision. One of the greatest challenges for congregational leaders in this phase is knowing how to respond with compassion to individuals who are upset or who challenge the new direction, while holding fast to the congregation's decision to live into a new vision of life together. The team's balcony perspective provides invaluable insight to the congregation's leaders as the leaders steer the church through uncharted, and sometimes rough, waters.

Renewal does not follow a script. Even with an overarching vision to guide you, the congregation's path to renewal will take twists and turns. Well-thought-out plans fail, or yield unexpected results. Sudden opportunities and emergencies arise.

A "balcony view" gives leaders a big-picture perspective that allows them to guide the congregation more effectively.

The balcony team helps the congregation progressively align all aspects of its life to serve the vision.

Changes frustrate or unnerve people, and they loudly demand that the congregation turn back. All along the way, situations will arise that tempt the congregation to veer off course or even to stop. The balcony team needs to be more committed to the congregation's aims than the congregation itself will be at times.

The balcony team's work ensures that all parts of congregational life are progressively realigned to serve the vision. As the team engages in this task, it always looks to do so in a way that supports its own and others' inner formation. Once again, the team providing primary leadership for renewal commits to learning how to embody what it desires for the rest of the congregation. "We become what we behold. We shape our tools and then our tools shape us." This quotation, attributed to educator and writer Marshall McLuhan, captures the importance of the attitudes and practices of those leading this final phase of renewal. What leaders do and the way they do it will be just as important as what they say. Balcony team members need to be aware of and take responsibility for the impact they have on the individuals and groups they work with.

We recommend that the team be made up of the senior pastor and three to five laity. These are often people who already hold key leadership positions and are familiar with the workings of the congregation. Whatever other roles team members currently serve in the congregation, they must commit first and foremost to serving the vision. Otherwise, they will subtly bend the vision to serve their other work. The membership of the balcony team will likely shift across the three to seven or more years it takes to live into the vision. This change is normal and can even be a helpful way of developing the leadership capacity of the laity and bringing needed gifts to the team.

In some congregations we've seen the pastor form this group without official recognition by the governing board. While a pastor can certainly benefit from the wisdom of an informal group of trusted advisors, renewal is best served when the group has official status. Formation by the governing board authorizes the group to carry out specific functions, minimizes the sense that the pastor "plays favorites," and keeps the ultimate responsibility for renewal with the congregation's governing board. We suggest that you look for people who are big-picture thinkers, who have excellent relational skills, who are trusted by the congregation and its leaders, who can work appropriately and creatively with conflict, and who themselves desire the envisioned future.

Here's how the formation of a balcony team took place at St. Paul's. Even before the vision process had been completed, the lead pastor could see that the congregation would need a balcony team. Without such a team, she knew, the congregation would assume she'd lead this last phase of renewal. That was tempting. She was eager to be part of the process and already had many opinions. At one point she considered having the staff take on the role. She knew that key laity would support that move. However, she also knew that the laity themselves needed to continue to take leadership of the congregation's renewal.

On the evening that the board approved the vision, the pastor brought up the need for a balcony team. That very night, the board began the third phase of renewal, appointing a balcony team of the board chair, the lay leader of the congregation, the chair of the personnel committee, and the lead pastor. Membership would rotate as new people assumed these offices.

The board charged the team with ensuring that the congregation made progress toward its vision, watching for and alerting the board and staff to issues that renewal raised in the congregation, reporting monthly to the board, and working as needed with other groups and committees to help them devise strategy. The board was clear: your job is not to make renewal

The balcony team strengthens the congregation by drawing the people into the work, rather than doing the work for them.

happen, but to coach us and the other groups as we work for that end.

The balcony team indeed needs to function as a coach for the congregation. Its goal is to help the congregation exercise its gifts and increase its strength, not to weaken the congregation by doing its work. The balcony team at Good Hope did it all. Composed of the lead pastor and the chairs of the ministry council, administrative board, and finance committee, this team single-handedly directed renewal. When a committee was faced with a challenge, the team was right there with the answer. When a new initiative was needed, the team developed the initial strategy and recruited the leadership needed to run it. Seven years later, the congregation felt like a new body. Prayer was central to its life. God was a felt presence. Members were reaching out to the community in ways they never had before. The congregation was living into its dream. And then the pastor left—and those on the balcony team stepped down. Although the new pastor was highly competent and much appreciated, many committees broke down. Across the past seven years, they'd never had to develop goals and strategies; the balcony team had taken care of it. Odd as it may sound, these very competent groups had no idea how to move forward. The balcony team always needs to do its work in a way that serves the health and strength of the person or group it's working with.

Six Key Areas Renewal Efforts Must Address

In watching and working with congregations addressing this third phase of renewal, we've noticed a tendency for them to focus their energy on starting new initiatives, while ignoring other aspects of congregational life. At the far extreme this mind-set takes the form of deeming new efforts "good" and existing programs "bad" and a foolish waste of time. Rather than feeling supported and empowered, congregants and existing committees get the impression that they're no longer seen as valued members of the community. This approach dismisses the very real ways God has long been working in and through the congregation. It gives rise to unnecessary resistance and fragments a congregation at the very time that the board is seeking to draw it into alignment.

Developing new initiatives is an important aspect of this phase of renewal, but five other areas of congregational life need attention, too, if the congregation is to continue developing an environment supportive of the vision and the long-term aims of renewal. The balcony team monitors these areas as the congregation and committees work to align themselves and their work with the vision. The six areas are:

- new initiatives
- existing ministries and programs
- congregational care
- spiritual and faith formation
- staff development
- lay leadership development

There is no set sequence in which these six areas must be addressed. You'll find they're related, and addressing one is often the doorway to discussing another. Any one of them, however, if *not* addressed, will cause serious problems. These areas support a congregation being *church*, a place where people are drawn into loving, life-giving relationship with God and one another. Each area contributes something unique to the formation of a generative,

---

A new vision typically results in new initiatives. The congregation needs to decide which will be addressed first and by whom.

---

transformative, healthy faith community. The balcony team needs to keep tabs on all six areas, coaching the congregation and its staff as they shift in the ways needed to serve the vision.

New Initiatives

Doing what you've always done gives you what you've always gotten, as the saying goes. Adjusting and improving what you already do will make a tremendous difference. But very likely, the vision you were granted calls for ministries, or strategies for doing ministry, that will be brand new for your congregation. Creating them will require imaginative thinking and innovative actions. Which strategies should the congregation address first? Which ones should wait? Who decides? And once a decision is made, who will be responsible for carrying it out?

These are big questions, and it's the balcony team's job to make sure that they get addressed. In some congregations, it will be clear from the vision process what the needed new initiatives are and which to focus on first. In those cases the governing board simply needs to assign responsibility to a group or individual, and the balcony team then keeps a supportive eye on it. In other congregations, it's not clear at all where to begin, and the governing board has turned its attention to other matters. In that case the balcony team might get things rolling by instigating a conversation with the board: "Our vision contains a brand-new area of ministry for us—working with immigrants. What's the first step that needs to be taken? How will that happen? Who will be responsible?" In some instances we've even seen the balcony team bring a recommendation about what the first key initiative might be. For the most part, though, the team's job is to raise questions rather than give answers—and when answers are found, to make sure they are then lived out.

Located in the heart of a metropolitan area, St. Paul's had for decades understood its mission as "serving Christ in the heart of the city." Across the previous twenty years, the downtown neighborhood surrounding the church had changed. The homeless population had dramatically increased, and the congregation had worked hard to respond faithfully. The congregation had changed, too. Each year the average age went up, and the size of the congregation and financial contributions went down. Drawing heavily on its endowment, the congregation also depended increasingly on staff both to provide care for members and to do outreach service projects in its name. With both the congregation and the endowment fund dwindling, members knew that the human and financial resources of the church would soon be exhausted.

In contemplating renewal, the congregation had become more acutely aware that other changes had taken place. The number of people working in nearby offices had tripled. The downtown core had become a fashionable place to live. Old buildings were being razed, and condos and apartments were going up. When the congregation envisioned God's hope for its ministry, it saw a place where people from very different life situations could find a bridge to one another and to God. The members shivered with anticipation when they thought about providing that bridge. This was what they felt was most needed by the world right now, and they were being given the opportunity to help it happen in their own city.

One of the vision's key elements was ministry by the people rather than by the staff. The problem was that while the members seemed truly to desire the development of a bridging congregation, no one had any idea how to do it. And so, for several months, nothing was done.

It took the balcony team to get things rolling. It proposed to the board that a group of members attend a training event that taught people how to establish a small-group ministry. The proposed event focused not only on developing an atmosphere of caring and generative community, but also on empowering people to be in mission. The governing board wholeheartedly endorsed the team's proposal. It seemed the right first step. The event would equip a group of the congregation's laity to create venues that would build bridges between people while nurturing each individual's spiritual growth. The board took it from there. Using endowment funds, it paid for a group of six laity and the pastor to attend the training. When they returned home, the six laypeople formed a new committee, blessed by the board. Across the next six months the committee would design and facilitate four short-term "test run" small groups, fostering relationships between diverse people as together participants explored questions of faith.

New initiatives can provide visible proof to the congregation that it is redirecting its energy along new lines. The renewal task force can help the congregation see these new efforts as needed additions rather than as replacements that sweep away the existing ministries and programs.

Existing Ministries and Programs

Your congregation already has a structure of committees and work teams. These groups have been working together for some time. Many, if not all, have an important part to play in the future congregation. At the same time, these groups have established patterns for how they function. They have certain tasks they're used to doing. Their challenge is realignment—shifting the parts of their work that aren't quite on target with the vision and stopping the activities and ways of relating that run counter to the congregation's new goals. Letting go of what doesn't serve the vision and its goals makes room for new strategies to be developed.

Committees left on their own can easily justify those plans that the members have a vested interest in. The balcony team

Groups responsible for existing ministries and programs must learn to look at their work through new lenses and align their efforts to support the vision.

can help existing groups look at their work through new lenses and develop criteria to help ensure that their work is aligned with the vision. Committee members who are attached to a particular ministry or project with which they identify may find this realignment of work painful. The very thought of shifting what they've always done or bringing ministries to an end can be disconcerting and leave them feeling unappreciated and misunderstood.

Phase 3 is a time of personal transitions as established patterns and programs are changed. The steps that helped people make the internal transitions required for visioning apply here, too:

- grounding themselves in God's vision for the congregation
- letting go of their preconceived notions of how the group best serves the vision
- opening themselves to God for direction
- sensing God's leading
- developing strategies

People do this inner work of transition at different rates. Some shift quickly, others very slowly. Almost all will be watching to see the way other people and other committees realign themselves and the outcome of that change. Until we believe that a new way of doing something is necessary or worthwhile, it's natural to hesitate. And even when we know that changes are needed and believe we're ready to make them, it's normal to feel grief. This is particularly true for a group and its members when

How can we provide care to our members in ways that allow the staff also to direct its time toward the congregation's new aims?

long-standing programs or annual events are discontinued. The balcony team can help by encouraging people to reflect on and celebrate how those activities once served well the congregation and God's aims.

Congregational Care

Members of a congregation expect their church to respond when they are in need. In most congregations members expect those needs to be met in specific ways by the pastor or other paid staff. Almost always, shifting the deployment of resources means changing how the staff spends its time. If relationships need to be developed with a new population group, the pastor and staff are often key players. This means that time may be diverted from longer-term members or constituents, leaving them feeling slighted or even abandoned.

While reaching out to new people, the staff and congregation must also develop ways to provide support to current members as they face life crises. The balcony team can help the staff and congregational leaders think through such questions as these: How do we provide care to our members while stretching in a new direction? How do we refuse to allow ourselves to be held hostage by those who might insist that care must be given in the way to which they have grown accustomed? How do we ensure that those in need of continuing care receive the support they need?

Failure to provide congregational care at a level perceived as adequate by members contributes to congregational conflict during renewal. Excited about the vision and encouraged by the enthusiasm of the congregation, the pastor and staff start giving themselves to developing new strategies. The time has to come from somewhere, and the first place many pastors look is visitation and member care. But members can grow resentful when they sense the withdrawal of a relationship that has become important, or experience minimal or no response to a personal crisis.

The pastor or staff person may indeed need to give less time to congregational care in order to support the congregation's new aims. But reallocating time needs to be done with an awareness of the impact it will have and with a plan for making sure that pastoral care needs are met. Even those supportive of new endeavors can become bitter when their needs are ignored.

It's easy for the pastor or staff person to react with anger or annoyance when a member complains, "The old folks who built this church just don't seem to matter any more. You've got to be young to count around here." Resist the temptation. Almost every complaint has at least some truth to it. If you can't seem to find it, ask yourself what the 2 percent of truth in the complaint is. This approach often opens the doorway to finding more wisdom there than you at first thought—usually far more than 2 percent.

The balcony team at Mullard Heights was well aware of the congregation's expectations that the pastor should provide ongoing as well as acute pastoral care to the aging congregation. This pressure had even been heightened by the congregation's recent move from having a full-time associate to having only one ordained pastor. Pastor Terry was committed to finding a new and better way of providing care for members. He knew they needed it. He also knew that he was not able to provide pastoral care in the way people had grown accustomed to receiving it while he was giving leadership to the new directions indicated by the vision.

Terry appreciated having the balcony team's support as he mulled over options. Its members were longtime, well-respected members of the congregation. He trusted their ability to sense what the congregation was thinking and feeling. And he knew that the congregation would be more willing to try a new system of providing care if it had these individuals' stamp of approval.

The team helped Terry think through the development of a small group of caring and trusted individuals who for three months would take over the work of regular visiting. The group would meet with the pastor each week for support and to keep him updated. They would call him in between if they learned of an emergency situation. During that time, at Terry's request, the balcony team members would keep their ears open. At the end of the three-month period, Pastor Terry and the group would assess the effectiveness of providing care this way and decide where to go from there. The balcony team can be helpful in keeping an ear tuned to what the congregation is saying and in encouraging the pastor and staff to find creative ways to provide care.

Spiritual and Faith Formation

Remember the signs of congregational health?

- continual spiritual formation as essential for everyone rather than an activity pursued by some

- relationships among people that embody Christ's *kin*-dom of God; relationships that are honoring, forgiving, loving, caring, mutual, and generative

- a deep, pervasive concern for the temporal and spiritual well-being of those beyond the doors of the church that manifests in action

Achieving God's vision for your congregation's future depends on its ability to reclaim and maintain these healthy practices. This work, which began in phase 1 and continued in phase 2, comes to fruition in phase 3. But it happens only with intention.

Think back on the Slinky metaphor that we introduced in chapter 2, and imagine supporting one end of a Slinky in the

The renewing congregation learns how to and continually creates venues for the spiritual and faith formation of its members.

palm of your left hand and the other end in the palm of your right, ends parallel to the floor. Imagine gently lifting one hand and then the other, feeling how the bulk of the Slinky shifts back and forth from end to end and from one hand to the other. Through your work up to this point, you have initiated new patterns, and you can already see the results. However, those shifts have not been anchored in place; nor have they moved through the entire system. It doesn't take much movement for a Slinky to return to its starting position; neither does it take much for the congregation to return to its former spiritually congealed state. That's generally what happens when the issues of spiritual and faith development are passed over in favor of addressing programmatic and administrative changes.

We see *spiritual* development as growth in our ability to experience and respond to God's Spirit. In that sense, most religions are spiritual. *Faith* development is a bit different, pointing to acquiring and living the understandings and practices of a particular religion's view of God, in this case Christianity. The bottom-line aim of renewal is creating a venue where both happen—the congregation senses and responds to God's Spirit, and people are introduced to and supported in understanding and practicing the teachings of Jesus Christ.

The balcony team plays an important role in the continued renewal of this area of congregational life, raising questions that the governing board and other groups often forget: What are the arenas in which spiritual and faith formation are taking place in depth? How are business and other group meetings supporting the formation of members? How much is God a felt presence in our congregation? How do we introduce people to the teachings and practices of Christianity? How do we support those who are already disciples in their ongoing development?

The balcony team encourages the development of strategies that foster the formation of the current members of the congregation. Individual members must continue working toward the transition of their own understandings and habits regarding church for the congregation to continue shifting:

- from growing the church to witnessing to faith
- from running the church to forming disciples
- from being people-led to being Spirit-led
- from participating in mission projects to having a God-given mission
- from fixing to creating

At St. Bartholomew's the balcony team caught word of the choir director's new way of running rehearsals. Excited by what they heard, they sat down with her for coffee. She said, "I have always believed that what the choir does is ministry and service. Through our music and our presence, we help the congregation connect with God and reflect on its call to the world. When the anthems we sing are also personal testimonies of the choir members' experiences of God's power and love, the music is transformative for listeners. It finally dawned on me that not everyone in the choir realizes that. So I've redesigned both our Thursday night and Sunday morning rehearsal time so that they intentionally prepare the group to be ministers of God's word, not just singers. For each anthem, we discuss when we each personally experienced that aspect of God or faith—why that makes a difference to us and what we want others to know about God as a result of our singing about it."

The team members conveyed to her the deeply appreciative comments they'd heard both from choir members and the congregation and asked if they could tell her story at the upcoming board meeting. The story provided a practical example of exactly what they were encouraging other leaders to do and why. In many instances the balcony team's role will be simply to notice the positive shifts taking place and to lift them up for others to see and learn from.

Staff Development

When a congregation's aims and trajectory shift, what's needed from pastor and staff also change. Just as committees must now determine when to say yes and no in light of the vision, so must staff members. Phase 3 requires the staff, just as surely as the congregation, to stretch itself, develop new muscles, and devise new strategies to support the congregation's new missional aims and the increased emphasis on spiritual and faith formation. Changes in congregational size demand additional shifts, as congregations of various sizes require different styles of leadership from the pastor and staff. If a significant change in size is part of your vision, we recommend that the balcony team educate itself in this area. The collection of articles in *Size Transitions in Congregations* (Alban Institute, 2001) is a good place to start.

We find that staff members often underestimate the changes that will be required of them. Although they may have encouraged the idea of renewal for years, staff people can find themselves in the mind-set that "it's the congregation that needs to change, not us." But staff members have patterns of working and relating that are just as deeply ingrained as those of the congregation. They know their job and, very likely, do it well. But when the nature of the congregation and its ministry changes, how people need to be equipped and supported changes too.

It's the congregation that, empowered by God's spirit, creates a new future. The vision comes to life as members' compassion for others' suffering and commitment to others' well-being compels them to Christlike action. The staff helps create the future by supporting the individuals and groups of the

The staff's primary job is equipping and empowering members for ministry.

congregation in finding their passion and giving themselves to the work called for by the new vision. When this is not how the staff functions, the way staff members spend their time needs to change. A congregation can't live into God's vision for it unless the people are supported by the staff in this way. The staff's primary job is equipping and empowering members for ministry.

The balcony team is an ideal group to reflect on what adaptations might be needed in how the staff functions and how staff members may be supported in making and leading the needed changes. Pastor Jim at First Lutheran was excited about the congregation's vision and shared with the rest of the balcony team the ideas he and the other member of the ministry staff had for implementing the vision. As they talked, the balcony team helped Jim become aware that he was seeing himself creating and doing the new ministries instead of supporting the congregation in creating and doing them. Learning to serve the vision through the development of the congregation's members remained Jim's biggest challenge. He enjoyed creating and participating in the various ministries himself. The balcony team played an important role in coaching Jim to move beyond his natural preference and to work with people in such a way that they developed the skills and confidence that he had.

Staffs that relate to members in equipping and empowering ways are developing disciples—people who have a continually transforming relationship with God and whose lives reflect the understandings and practices of Jesus Christ.

Lay Leadership Development
The sixth area this phase of renewal must address is the development of lay leadership. While related to the preceding discussion of staff development, it is different enough and ignored

frequently enough to warrant a separate discussion. In a healthy congregation clergy and laity exercise leadership jointly. Both take responsibility for developing individuals as disciples of Christ and the organization as the body of Christ.

As current leaders help the congregation live into the vision, they need to do so in a way that develops the leadership of the congregation's members. Leadership is not the domain of a few chosen individuals but the call of each person in a congregation. As we noted in chapter 2, one definition of leadership is the ability to influence people toward a particular end or result. A congregation's vision provides a picture of the life-giving result God intends it to have. That dream becomes a reality only as members lead others in the congregation and community into that future. To do that, members need to be mindful of the influence they want to have on others and be able to make adjustments when their attitudes and behaviors have the opposite effect.

Some members will be called to take on specific leadership roles within the congregation. Of those, some will already be skilled leaders either within the congregation or in other arenas. They need only to transfer their skills to the task at hand. Other people, although they have never served in a leadership capacity before, will also find themselves called. These newly designated leaders will need training and support. The balcony team needs to champion the development of a system for the training and continuing support of lay leaders.

The continual surfacing and development of new leaders is key to the ongoing transformation of the congregation. New voices bring fresh perspectives. When ethnic, economic, or generational demographic shifts are part of the transformation, the composition of the congregation's leadership needs to reflect

The congregation must address ways of developing leaders rather than just electing them.

both the new and any additional sought-after diversity. When the laity own the vision and can develop strategies that move the congregation toward it, they are functional disciples, no longer dependent on the pastor and staff to do their work for them. The development of lay leadership magnifies the impact a congregation can have while ensuring that renewal will last beyond the current pastor's tenure.

The committees at St. Paul's leaned heavily on the staff to design and implement ministries. The education committee was a case in point. For several years, the committee had hired a series of interns to develop and provide leadership for the education program. Committee members helped out as needed, but their primary responsibility was to gather monthly to hear progress reports. The form and content of the education program varied as interns came and went. The food-bank group operated in a similar way. The program was coordinated and run by a paid staff person; committee members took turns helping to bag and distribute food.

A key component of the vision was ministry by the members, so the balcony team knew that the committees would have to be weaned from their dependency on staff. Internal leadership needed to be strengthened. This process was more difficult than the team had first imagined. Staff members were used to taking the shortcut of doing the work themselves. It was far more complicated and time consuming to teach members how to do it and then to encourage them when they grew frustrated or unsure. The change was not easy for the members either. They were not used to being depended on so heavily and were reluctant to accept leadership roles. Three years later, however, much had changed. Members now led all of the congregation's ministries.

It will take time for your congregation to make this change. Both staff and members may find the shift challenging. We encourage you to stay with the effort. The balcony team can help the congregation's leaders stay focused on addressing this work.

Bottom Line

The most provocative vision in the world won't lead to a changed congregation if its members don't act on what they've said they want. Renewal will touch every aspect of congregational life, requiring the realignment of existing ministries and the creation of new ones. It will shift what staff members do and how they do it, and it will develop the leadership of the laity. Renewal will change how the pastor and congregation provide care to members and how the members care for one another. All these changes serve the formation of people's spiritual and faith lives, so that they might be Christ's loving, healing, and empowering presence in the world.

The Unique Challenges of Phase 3

In chapter 2 we discussed the challenges of congregational renewal. You will likely experience every one of them during this phase. In addition, three other challenges seem to arise more often in phase 3 than in the earlier two.

We Want to Go Back

Shortly after the Hebrew people packed their belongings and walked away from their place of captivity in Egypt, they grew fearful. "What have you done to us? . . . [I]t would have been better for us to serve the Egyptians than die in the wilderness." (Exod. 14:11–12). The fear and complaints persisted through much of their journey. Having let go of one way of life, they had not yet found their way to the new and promised one. Moments of fear alternated with expressions of hope. Their fear took form not as self-disclosing statements such as, "I'm feeling afraid," but as blaming and demands: "What have you done to us? We want to go back!"

Expect phase 3 to be punctuated by such moments. People became engaged in the vision process without realizing the full impact of the choices they were making. How could they know until they started walking the path? Some unconsciously assumed that they could have it all—the way things used to be *and* the new future. When people realize that saying yes to new endeavors really does mean saying no to some of their existing practices, they begin to draw back.

Some will have concerns about the impact of the shifts on them personally. Others will be concerned for the congregation and what it has historically stood for. While wanting the congregation to move into the future, people will be protective of what has been held important in the past. These concerns may manifest as resistance to new endeavors or proposed changes to the building or existing programs, or as volatile comments in a meeting that seem to come from nowhere.

Anticipate resistance. We've found that helping people become aware of, articulate, and work through their feelings that "this is hard" or "it's not what I expected" minimizes blow-ups. Blow-ups are often the result of a person's either not being aware of his or her growing frustration, or of feeling as though nobody is listening. Leaders need to learn to listen in ways that leave people feeling heard.

When blow-ups do occur, many situations simply require creating space for people to ventilate their emotions safely. Here's what we've found can help. Breathe. Listen compassionately. Rather than making the person feel "wrong," listen for the truth embedded in his or her statement. You may be surprised by the wisdom hidden in comments you'd ordinarily dismiss. Pull back to a balcony perspective and ask: what insights does this flare-up offer on what's happening in the congregation on a larger scale? Seek to understand the person's underlying concerns for himself or herself and the congregation, but at the same time hold firm to the vision surfaced by the congregation. The congregation took an enormous risk in saying yes to God's vision. Champion the vision while finding ways to help fearful people discover their place in the new future and their role in helping the congregation blaze a path.

We Need a Break

At some point in time, one or more of the leaders will likely express how much the congregation has pushed itself during the last months or years: "It's time for a breather, time to let people take a much-needed rest."

As you look more deeply into such comments, you may find that it's the leaders, those who have shouldered much of the responsibility, who are tired. Feeling exhausted, they project their own feelings onto the entire congregation. When this is the case, a breather for those leaders rather than a congregational hiatus is indicated. The challenge is honoring the need for particular leaders to rest while not allowing their individual needs to dictate the pace for the entire congregation. Newton's first law of inertia teaches us that an object in motion tends to stay in motion, and an object at rest tends to stay at rest. It's much easier to keep a congregation moving than to get it moving again once it has stopped. The challenge is to encourage leaders to take the breaks they need, while maintaining the momentum of renewal.

Ironically, at the very time certain key leaders may be feeling weary, others in the congregation may be experiencing a heightened sense of energy. A key strategy for the continuation of renewal is encouraging tired leaders to take the break they need while turning to and empowering others to step into leadership. Renewal is not a sprint. We don't think of it even as a marathon. Renewal is a long-distance relay, run by many people over a span of years. In developing lay leaders, you prepare people to receive and run with the baton of leadership. But new leaders can't take over unless those who have been carrying the baton let go of it. One of the challenges facing leaders is handing off the leadership to others who are ready and eager to step forward. Developing relationships between current and future leaders can help develop the trust that allows these handoffs to go more smoothly. When leaders are unwilling to let go, the balcony team or governing board may need to intervene.

Renewal is not a marathon but a long-distance relay, run by many people over a span of years.

We Have the Answer

As renewal progresses successfully, it's tempting to codify the journey you've taken. You know what worked, and as a result you've developed certain patterns and loyalties. "Now we know the *right* way to lead renewal and the *right* processes to use." Openness and curious searching are replaced by certainty and knowing. Without realizing it, we slip, as did those before us, into institutionalizing what had once been a movement. The moment we do that, we begin killing the spirit of renewal.

God is always inviting a congregation to step into a new future. God also invites people to discover and design anew the processes for getting there. As your congregation continue its work, keep an eye on the future, but be as present as you can with one another. God is with you. The answers you will need and the transformation you seek will be found as you turn to one another and to God.

Discussion Questions

1. How are you feeling as you anticipate transforming a dream for your congregation into reality? How are your feelings similar to and different from those of others working on this renewal effort? What is your energy level for the work ahead?

2. Review the characteristics and skills the authors recommend for members of your balcony team. What people come to mind as you think about these traits?

3. Look at the list of six areas of congregational life that need to be aligned as a congregation undergoes renewal.

Which area are you most concerned about, and why? What thoughts do you have about how that area might most effectively be addressed?

4. Which of the three challenges to renewal do you suspect are at work in your congregation? What signs do you see? How do you think your congregation's leaders might respond most helpfully?

5. How do you sense God inviting your congregation to step into a new future in spite of the challenges you face?

6
A Primer on Planning

We encourage you to dream God's wild and seemingly impossible dreams. We want you to have more than just the dreams, however. We want you to have the reality, which comes to pass as you determine which aspects of the dream to work on first, devise strategies to realize them, and then act on what you've said you wanted.

Congregations are getting better and better at dreaming, and so are clergy. We celebrate the growing openness to dialogue and story as a means of transformation and take delight in the wide variety of tools and processes available to help groups connect and discern. Unfortunately, as church leaders swing away from old-school strategic planning models to embrace a more communal form of group discernment, some key skills are getting lost. It's a case of the baby getting thrown out with the bathwater.

Some church leaders cringe at the word "planning" and dismiss the very idea, suggesting instead gathering in radical openness to God until transformation naturally takes place. Others practice a lockstep, secular approach to planning that allows no room for God, for transformative conversation, or for creativity. In our experience both of these approaches miss the mark. The first renounces our responsibility as God's creative partners, putting the onus entirely on God to make the dream come true. The second dismisses God's role and the power of a connected community. We find that the most successful congregations use a combination of both, and this is what we mean when we say "planning."

Planning is fundamentally a way of creating things: a garden, a vacation, a new phase of life, a piece of art. Creating a painting, a sculpture, or a symphony requires a constant cycle of planning. What wants to be created? What's here now? What needs to be done next? Whether you're creating art or a renewed congregation, the aim of planning and carrying out that plan is creating something that previously did not exist.

Renewal planning is an intentional joining with God in God's continuing process of creation to bring new hope and healing to the world. The goals that we name and to which we give ourselves must be worthy, serving that larger purpose which we have discerned to be God's purpose. At the same time, the results must be those that we truly want; otherwise we turn aside when our attention is diverted or the work gets hard. We must allow ourselves to be formed by the mind and heart of God, so that we want the same things that God wants. Our goals then are both worthy of our time and energy and important enough to us that we'll make them our primary focus. Pursuing worthy goals that we truly want gives our lives meaning and brings life to others.

Accepting our responsibility as co-creators with God means knowing and using some kind of planning process, some method for turning a dream into a reality. For some people, planning comes naturally. As soon as an idea comes into their minds, they're making it happen. They may even engage in the steps so intuitively, so unconsciously, that they don't even realize what they're doing is a form of planning. For other people, and for many groups, planning is neither intuitive nor easy. In fact, for some, planning is a dreaded process that brings on a feeling of heaviness. Particularly if you are in the latter camp, we encourage you to view planning as a way of serving God, of bringing into being something God wants to create through you.

Planning can take many forms that on the surface may look very different from one another. The Appreciative Inquiry process, with its emphasis on storytelling and its premise that "what we dream about is what we enact," would seem to be miles away from classic strategic planning. However, the steps of Appreciative Inquiry—*discover, dream, design, deliver*—are the same fundamental steps of strategic planning. The difference between the two is the style, how those steps are approached. There are many "labeled" planning methods to choose from. We believe that today's congregations are best served by a collaborative approach to planning that brings out the best of the congregation and uses it as a springboard for designing what's next. We've seen that achieved through a variety of planning forms. Successful planning models seem to hold these five elements in common:

- Develop a clear sense of what you want to achieve and a commitment to achieve it.

- Honestly assess where you're starting from.

- Design steps that will move you from where you are to where you want to be.

- Take those steps.

- Assess whether your actions are getting you where you want to go and then make adjustments as needed.

Renewal will not happen in your church without your mastering some kind of planning process that incorporates these five elements. One of the most frequent laments we hear from clergy and congregations is that they don't know what do after they dream. This chapter gives you the specific steps of the particular process we teach and use most often in our work. This methodology can be used for projects as small as making the entryway to the church more inviting, or as large as surfacing the congregation's vision. The steps are the same for both. We'll give an overview of the planning process and then examine each of the steps in detail, giving an example of how a specific church used this approach.

An Overview of the Process

When we help groups plan, we lift up the importance of each goal's being a worthy goal, one that serves the ultimate purposes of the congregation and of God. So, as you get ready to plan, have conversations that remind you of the purpose of your group and what your work is supposed to serve. Listen together for what God might want as a result of your work on the task at hand, sharing what you each hear. The goals your group ultimately articulates, even if they are small, need to serve God's overarching call to your congregation.

Once you're clear about the larger purpose you want to serve, here's one way of developing a plan:

1. Identify what you want to accomplish. Describe it in a way that is specific, measurable, achievable, relevant, and time-bound.

2. Determine your starting point. What assets do you have to work with? What challenges are present?

3. Identify the major components of the work required to move from here to there.

4. Test the worthiness and power of the goal. Do you really want it? Is it important? If the answer is no, go back to step 1.

5. Develop an overall time line, identifying the sequence of the major components and how they are related. When does each need be started? When does each have to be completed to allow progress on the others?

6. If you are planning with a group, identify who in the group will oversee each component.

7. Create a plan for accomplishing each of the major components, using the sequence of steps listed above.

8. Determine how the group will assess its progress, make adjustments, and keep itself accountable for staying on track and on schedule.

9.   Proceed with the work, adjusting your plans as needed.

The steps of the planning process can at first seem complex and even overwhelming. Breaking the work into simple steps, however, makes it more doable. Planning ensures that a group achieves results that reflect its dreams.

How to Build a Plan

Below we have taken each of the nine steps and explained them in more detail. We also offer an example of how one church worked through each step in developing child-care services.

Step 1: Identify What You Want to Accomplish

Arriving at a particular destination requires more than simply getting in the car and beginning to drive. You must have certain information about that destination to get where you want to go.

So where do you want to go? What do you want to accomplish? What do you want to create? What results do you want to achieve? This is the place to start. In what follows, we'll use the word "goal" to refer to what you want to accomplish.

Your goal needs to be what is commonly called in business literature a SMART goal. SMART stands for *specific, measurable, attainable, relevant,* and *time-bound*. Some people shy away from business language and principles. We believe in gathering and using best practices and what we've learned from a variety of disciplines, however. The SMART goal concept helps you turn a dream into a concrete picture you can plan for.

The goal must be *specific*. You are able to describe it, paint a picture of it.

- What do we want to accomplish?
- Who is involved?

- What are the benefits of accomplishing this goal?

The goal must be *measurable*. You are able to know when you have achieved it or not yet achieved it.

- How much? How many? By when?
- How do we know when the goal is accomplished?

The goal must be *attainable*. Though it may make you stretch, it is realistically achievable.

- Given our resources, and the circumstances of time and situation, is this goal realistic?
- Even though we don't yet see how, do we believe we can achieve it?
- Is the goal too big? Not big enough?

The goal must be *relevant*. Not only is the goal possible, but in addition, the people believe it's fundamentally important and worth working for.

- What makes this goal worthy of our time and efforts?
- What is the immediate larger goal that this specific goal serves?
- How does this goal serve the larger vision of the congregation?

The goal must be *time-bound*. Specific dates are named to which you hold yourself accountable.

- When must this goal be completed?
- How might events on the larger church calendar affect our work and this completion date?

Trinity Church is located in an older neighborhood of modest homes in a city of about 300,000. The neighborhood is shifting as young families purchase the houses that come up for sale. Trinity's vision calls for the congregation to connect with these younger families and to offer a setting for faith development. The congregation currently consists of adults whose own adult children live elsewhere. No child care is offered during worship or educational events.

One component of Trinity's plans for renewal is to provide child care during worship and other events. In January, the governing board named a five-person child-care task force to develop and implement a plan to have child care available for worship by the first Sunday of Advent. The completion date coincided with a major outreach effort to the neighborhood that would begin with Advent and lead up to Christmas. Therefore, the task force had ten months to carry out its assignment.

Trinity had not provided child care for many years. Feeling a bit overwhelmed, the members began by reminding themselves of the relevance of the assignment. For the planned Advent/ Christmas outreach to be successful, child care was essential. And they knew that the outreach ministry being planned was a key step in Trinity's ability to connect with the younger families in the neighborhood. Their work could really help the congregation make its dream come true.

Several task force members had children living in other cities who themselves had infants and younger children. They knew many of the expectations younger families had regarding child care. That knowledge helped the task force members envision the results they wanted. They knew that the facility had to be bright, welcoming, well-equipped, and safe. They knew parents had to feel confident that it was a good place to leave their infants and younger children. And it had to be a place the children looked forward to coming to.

They envisioned a space for infants in cribs adjacent to but separated from a space for toddlers. They decided to plan for six infants and an area that would accommodate twelve toddlers. The space for toddlers would offer a variety of activities. Staffing would meet established standards for those numbers.

The task force quickly realized that this was a huge undertaking. Preparing the physical space would take significant planning and work. Furnishing the center would be a major project. And staffing would be a key issue. The group also recognized that the costs of completing the project could be significant. It would be difficult, but the task force believed itself up to the challenge.

It knew that the assigned completion date was the first Sunday of Advent. The task force wanted several "test run" Sundays before that Sunday. Its members decided they would set an earlier date, the first Sunday in November, as their completion date.

The task force named its goal:

Trinity's child-care center will be open November 1. It will nurture the physical, emotional, and spiritual well-being of the children it serves. It will accommodate six infants in cribs in one room with space for twelve toddlers in an adjacent room. The rooms will be clean, bright, and well furnished, and the decor will be age-appropriate. The facility and the staffing will meet current standards for church child-care facilities. The center and its staff will instill confidence in parents and be enjoyable to the children.

Step 2: Determine Your Starting Point

To chart a course that will take you to your destination, you must accurately identify your departure point. For each aspect of the goal, identify what now exists. What assets do you have? What challenges do you face?

Groups often neglect these questions in the planning process and then find themselves in trouble. You can't accurately determine what needs to be done if you don't know what you're working with. Naming current reality in this step doesn't mean describing everything about the current state of the congregation. Focus only on what is relevant to the goal.

Enthusiasm for a project or eagerness to get started can lead a group to overlook important strengths or dismiss less-than-favorable conditions. Identifying the skills and resources the group has to work with creates a pool of assets the group can draw from. Naming the known challenges up front allows the group to plan for how to deal with them.

The Trinity child-care task force looked at its goal and wondered what it had to work with. Was anyone in the church versed in the physical, emotional, and spiritual needs of infants and toddlers? Who in the church might be familiar with current standards for child care? What space was available, and what was the condition of that space? What funding was available for the project? What furnishings or equipment might the church already have? Who in the church had a connection with a neighborhood parent who might be willing to provide some advice about what local parents expected?

Once the task force figured out the right questions to ask, it went to work finding some answers about the assets it had at its disposal and the challenges it would have to deal with. The pastor was willing to talk with the group about the spiritual needs of children. She had a friend who could provide information about the emotional and physical needs of children in the age groups the center would serve. Trinity had several unused rooms that were easily accessible from the entryway to the church. Though these rooms were located on the ground floor, they did not have access directly to the outdoors. Neither restrooms nor running water was available in the rooms. The lighting was dim, although the rooms did have large windows.

The church had no furnishings or equipment that could be used, such as cribs or toys. The task force members did not know current child-care standards and policies, nor did they know anyone in the church who knew. Nor did anyone seem to know any of the nearby families that might advise the group.

Though the center would be open only on Sunday and for congregational events, the board took the issue of staffing quite seriously. It asked that the task force propose a system for supervising the center's staff and that any paid position be approved by the finance committee prior to hiring.

The task force noted that the funding approved by the board seemed adequate. A number of men in the church were skilled in carpentry, plumbing, and electrical work, and over the years they had gladly offered their services for church projects. Most of the work could be done for the cost of materials.

The team also discussed concerns it had heard expressed by some members about the cost of the project and worries that the children would be loud and would run wild. The task force noted that while the board was supportive, the congregation at large had mixed feelings.

Step 3: Identify the Major Components of the Work

Now that you're clear about your starting point, you may feel ready to jump in and start doing the work. Your efforts so far have likely surfaced many of the important tasks to be addressed. Some, however, may still lie hidden. Before proceeding, reflect on the entirety of the work before you. With the starting place and the goal in mind, what are the major components that must be addressed if you're to get the results you want? Don't discuss how each might be done or who would be responsible at this point. Simply list the components. You'll develop a plan for each in step 7.

Looking at both the goal you've written and your description of current reality, step back and ask:

- Are there physical issues to address such as space, equipment, or renovation? If so, what are they?

- Does the project require hiring or recruiting people to staff it?

- Are there financial issues to address? If so, what are they?

- Might the project raise issues with the congregation or community? If so, what are they?

- From within the congregation, what official approval will be needed for the project?

- Are there legal issues, permits that must be secured? If so, what are they?

- Does the project involve selecting or preparing a curriculum? If so, what kind?

- Is specialized training needed? If so, what kind?

- Are there public-relations or advertising issues to address? What are they?

Again, resist the temptation at this point to jump into actual planning. Your first task is to look at what these questions surfaced and to identify the four to eight major components of the work. This process breaks the project down into manageable chunks and ensures that the important factors are addressed, without their getting lost in minutiae.

The Trinity task force identified the following major components of the goal:

- *Renovating the space.*

- *Furnishing the center.*

- *Researching child-care standards and policies.*

- *Staffing the center.*

- *Coordinating and communicating with the governing board and congregation.*

- *Recommending to the board a plan for continuing oversight of the center and its staff.*

- *Preparing the congregation for children.*

Step 4: Test the Worthiness and Power of the Goal

You have defined your goal, identified the current reality in rela-tion to the goal, and named the major components of the work. Step back and look at the goal and what must be done to achieve it. Is the goal worthy of the time and effort it will take? Do you want the results strongly enough to give yourself to the work? Do you feel called to this task? Individual group members need to ask themselves these questions, as does the group as a whole.

A goal is worthy when it serves something larger you're trying to accomplish. In the case of a congregation, a goal is worthy to the extent that it ultimately serves the congregation's vision. When looked at in isolation, some goals might seem mundane. But larger goals are dependent on the completion of smaller goals. A goal's worthiness is found not in its stand-alone value but in its contribution to larger goals and greater purposes.

Sometimes a group can become so drawn up in the details of planning that its members lose sight of the larger purpose of their work. They invest time and energy reaching for results that don't serve the congregation's larger purposes. Test again the worthiness of the goal you are working on. If the goal lacks worthiness, now is the time to address it. Your group may have power either to adjust or to abandon the goal. If that preroga-tive lies elsewhere, the group may need to go back to the source of the goal and recommend that it be reshaped or dropped.

Examine whether the goal still has power for you. You may fully believe in the importance of the goal but believe that you are not the person called to work on it. How compelling does the goal seem to you? If you have reservations, ask yourself whether something is standing in the way that could be ad-dressed. If you don't want to give yourself to this project, now is the time to declare that. Your honesty says nothing about the importance of the goal for the church. Nor does your unwillingness to work on this goal necessarily reflect on your willingness to give yourself fully to other goals. If this work is not for you, say so now. Lukewarm commitments are the bane of the church.

The Trinity task force now realized just how big this project was. Were its members really willing to take it on? The members reminded themselves of the larger congregational goal of outreach to younger families in the community. They all believed that this initiative was important. They wanted the Advent/Christmas outreach to be successful. The only way that could happen was by making sure that child care for little ones was available. Failure to provide high-quality child care would dramatically impede the success of the larger goals of the congregation.

As the task force discussed this project, it became clear that the members had already developed a deep personal investment in creating the child-care center. People's enthusiasm had grown as they had worked together. While the work certainly was daunting, they felt eager to begin and grateful to be a part of this effort.

Step 5: Develop the Basic Time Line for the Overall Work

Some components will probably need to be completed before others can be started. A time line orders the work so that all the pieces fit together and the work flows smoothly. Later on, you'll be fleshing out this time line. Your task in this step is simply to sequence the major components.

Look at each of the major components and decide how they should be ordered. Are there some that must be completed before others can be started? What completion dates must be set so that the various components and the project are completed on time? Develop a time line that gives the completion date for each major component of the plan.

The child-care task force wrote each major component of the project in large letters on separate pieces of paper. The chairperson then taped the pieces of paper on the whiteboard in the meeting room.

Looking at all seven components together, the group discussed which ones would have to be finished before others could be started. The task force identified "researching child-care policies and standards" as the component that the others hinged on. That would need to be completed first. The chairperson moved the piece of paper listing that task to the left side of the board.

Starting with that one, the group worked its way though the list of components. For each it asked, "When does this component need to be completed for other work to proceed smoothly?" As the group members went through the list, they ordered the components, assigning each a date by which it needed to be completed. By the end of the discussion, the seven components were arranged on the board in order of their completion dates.

Step 6: Assign Responsibilities

Worthy goals and detailed plans alone accomplish nothing. People must actually do the work if they're to achieve the desired results. Congregations make two common mistakes Leaders assume that people will see the importance of the work and automatically step forward to see that it is done. Or leaders make decisions about who they think should do the work and pressure those individuals into taking responsibility for the tasks. Neither method works. Both result in unaccomplished goals.

Planning requires that you identify both the work to be done and who will do that work. When assigning responsibilities, the group needs to make sure that the people being held responsible for tasks know the scope of the tasks and are truly willing to take them on.

The Trinity task force members decided among themselves who would be responsible for each major component—not that these individuals would do the work alone, but that they would be the ones to shepherd a particular aspect of the project. Jim volunteered to colead the remodeling if someone would join him. Annie raised her hand. She'd felt drawn to that component of the work, but hadn't wanted to take it on by herself. Joyce and Andrea followed their example and decided they'd colead

furnishing the center. Each person on the task force took respon-
sibility for a component of the project.

Step 7: Develop a Plan for Each Major Component

In step 3 you broke the work of achieving the goal into its major components. In step 6 an individual or a team assumed responsibility for each. Now in step 7 you need to develop a plan for each component, using the same steps you just used—setting a SMART goal, naming your starting point, and so forth. Continuing to break the work down into small components makes the work manageable and the goal achievable.

As a time line is developed for work on each of the components, those time lines are brought together and integrated. The group responsible for the overall management of the project monitors the progress toward the goal so that issues that need attention are discovered early and addressed. This attentiveness keeps the work moving.

The child-care task force discussed the best way to develop a plan and time line for each of the components. It was clear that detailed planning for the renovation component couldn't take place until Jim and Annie had had a chance to gather a team and learn about building codes and any pertinent standards for child-care areas. This was true for other components of the project as well.

The task force decided that during the next week each leader or pair of leaders would develop the first steps of a plan for their component of the project. The task force members would meet in one week to share the initial plans and to check with each other for any conflicts or points of overlap. As detailed plans and time lines were developed for each component, leaders would bring them to the task force for inclusion in a master time line.

A week later, the task force members shared what they saw as the first steps of their plan. This conversation helped group members to identify aspects of the work that had been overlooked and to understand better how the various components needed to fit together.

One task force member took responsibility to develop a master time line and to keep it updated. This chart allowed the task force to see the flow of the work and how each component helped the project move to completion. Task force members found the chart extremely helpful when talking with the governing board, committees, or congregation members. People seemed to be able to understand the project better when they could see a visual representation on paper. The chart answered many of the questions people seemed to have. "What about . . . ? Have you thought about . . . ? When will you . . . ?" The task force members had thought the chart would be a helpful tool for their work, but they were surprised at what an effective communication tool the time-line chart turned out to be.

Step 8: Establish a Way to Hold Yourself Accountable

Once a plan has been developed, it's important to set up a system to keep things on track. People and groups don't always complete agreed-upon tasks by an agreed-upon date—and for many reasons. People may have thought they were totally capable of carrying out a task but then learned that they did not have the needed skills. Perhaps other projects diverted their attention. Personal or family illness can prevent someone from following through. Leaders need to know this information as soon as possible, for the sake of the project but also for the support of the individuals involved.

Knowing that particular parts of the work have not been completed as expected is the only way a team can hold itself accountable for achieving the goal on time. An accountability system gives leaders the information they need to make adjustments and to stay on top of what's being done and what's gotten dropped. The idea here is not to punish or humiliate people who drop the ball, but to make sure that a dropped ball is picked up and moved on before it becomes a problem. A structure for accountability should be developed for each sub-phase of a project as well as for the project as a whole.

These structures keep the project moving, but they can also keep the leaders in touch with what's going on in the lives of the people working on the project. Establishing regular times to check in with those leading the various components provides opportunities for connection and ongoing support.

The task force decided to meet every other week for the duration of the project. This schedule would allow them to function as an accountability group as well as a management team. Knowing they would be updating each other regularly would encourage them to stay current with their work. It would also allow them to assess the overall progress of the project and to make adjustments as needed.

As the work progressed, the group members found that these regular meetings provided invaluable support. They prayed together, discussed the challenges they faced, and celebrated each milestone. Although they had known each other before this project, the nature of their biweekly meetings brought them closer together.

Step 9: Adjust Your Plans as Needed

As work on a project progresses, the unexpected happens. New information emerges, unforeseen situations arise, or the work doesn't produce the expected results. When those shifts take place, plans often need to shift too. Such readjustment is a normal part of developing and working out a plan. Expect it. Create plans, but be ready to adjust those plans when needed. Don't make the mistake of being more attached to your plans than you are to your goal.

Assessing progress at regular intervals will keep you aware of emerging developments and allow you to make adjustments as needed. If a problem seems to be cropping up, you want to know about it as soon as possible. If caught and addressed early, most situations don't become problems but simply remain curves in the path you hadn't anticipated. It's not uncommon for these adjustments and detours to bring unexpected benefits. And for those situations that are truly *problems*, the sooner you do something about them, the better.

Across the months, the task force members developed the habit of reflecting on a series of questions each time they met.

- *How is work progressing? Are we on schedule?*
- *Are we getting the results we expected? If not, what needs to shift?*
- *What challenges have arisen since we last met?*
- *What opportunities have opened up?*
- *Where are we seeing God at work?*

The plans they made generally worked well. At times adjustments needed to be made. Most adjustments were simple and were made by the smaller sub-groups themselves. But as standards for child care were researched, it became clear that the available space would allow for only four infants and eight toddlers. These numbers were different from those envisioned in the goal and required the entire task force to sign off on the change.

Some Final Thoughts

It is through planning that a group determines where it wants to go, how it is going to get there, and how it will know when it has arrived. Whatever method of planning you use, remember that two of the primary aims of a congregation are the spiritual formation of its members and the transformation of the world.

How you plan should serve both. Creating and implementing plans should ideally be holy encounters as people work with each other and with God.

We've pushed the accomplishment of tasks very hard in this chapter. But we would be remiss if you came away with the idea that congregational planning is only about accomplishing the task. Groups that mindfully create something out of nothing and bring order out of chaos participate with God in creation. Creating with mindful intention transforms a group and the individuals in the group. People come away closer to one another and more sure of God's presence. They have an air about them that says, "We, with God, can do anything." And quite often, they can.

Congregational groups and teams accustomed to planning together seem to do so effortlessly. The steps we outlined are present, but done fluidly and naturally. We assure you that it wasn't always that way for them. Have you ever watched someone learning to dance for the first time? Every movement is tense and awkward. Each step is a half-beat fast or slow. A man of our acquaintance who was learning to dance asked a partner for advice on how to improve. She cocked her head thoughtfully and replied, "Try to move more like a cat and less like a cow." Several years later, he has become an excellent dancer, and his movements are indeed smooth and catlike. Although his holding a mental picture may have helped, the shift happened primarily because he practiced the movements over and over until they became second nature.

As you read through the planning process outlined above, you may have thought it sounded cumbersome and unnatural. It can certainly appear that way at first. If you've never been very successful at planning, your first attempts may seem awkward. That's normal. We recommend that you practice on smaller goals before tackling enormous ones. Above all, keep before you the intent to meet God in the process. It is God's dream you are dreaming and God's hope and healing your work is making manifest in the world. Be present with the people you work with and open to hearing their ideas and sharing your own. Be curious about what God is doing through you and, like those travelers on the road to Emmaus, you may very likely recognize God present in your midst.

The Carpenter and the Unbuilder

Even Our Brokenness

The more the carpenter and the unbuilder traveled together, the more the carpenter understood what it meant to build a house. He understood something about his insecurity, his fearfulness, and how hard it was to trust when you couldn't quite see your destination. And the more he became aware of these weaknesses, the more often he felt guilty and angry with himself. He felt bad when he was building a house; and even when he moved on, the memory of the last house he had built—or maybe even the house before that—continued to haunt him.

One day after he had decided to leave a particularly nice little place he had built, the unbuilder could see that the carpenter was very discouraged. As they were leaving the little house and the valley in which he had built it, the unbuilder stopped.

"Look back for a moment," the unbuilder said gently.

As the carpenter turned around, he saw his former home and, in the distance, a woman. She had just entered the valley from the other side. She looked very tired, and she was alone. In fact, she looked as if she could hardly take another step. However, when she saw his recently abandoned dwelling, she seemed to gain new strength. With quickening steps she moved to the house and knocked on the door. Receiving no answer, she went inside.

The carpenter looked at the unbuilder for an explanation. The unbuilder spoke carefully, "Once you have left your original home and accepted the invitation to dinner, every step on the journey links you to all who are on their way to dinner. Sometimes the home that you build out of your need and then let go of or leave behind, can help another traveler Not everyone can do what you do. Not everyone will welcome someone like me. The king cares for his travelers in many ways. That woman was about to turn around and abandon the journey. Your former home will provide the shelter she needs until she is ready to resume her journey."

At that moment the carpenter felt as if a great weight, or sorrow, left him; he turned and walked over the crest of the hill, more eager than ever to be on his way.

Home

The carpenter and the unbuilder had been traveling together for quite a while, and for a long time the carpenter had not built much of anything. Every now and again he made something to stay in, but it was only for overnight and just enough to protect himself from some particularly bad weather. While this pleased him, another thought had begun to bother him. It seemed to the carpenter that he had been traveling long enough that they should have gotten to the castle by this time. Yet the unbuilder never seemed to mention such things. The carpenter decided to raise the issue.

"How much longer until we get to the castle?" he asked.

"I can't tell," came the reply.

"You can't tell?" He wasn't sure if he should be annoyed or afraid. "Are we lost?" he inquired.

"No."

"Well then, do you know where the castle is?"

"Yes," the unbuilder offered again.

"Then why can't you tell me how much longer until we get there? I haven't built many houses recently. I have stayed on the road. Surely you can tell me if we are close—or at least closer?"

"I can't tell."

"You know, but you can't tell?"

"Yes, I know, but I can't tell. This is one truth, one awareness you must discover for yourself."

"Is there no help you can give me? No word of advice, comfort, or encouragement?" asked the carpenter.

"I am permitted to give you one bit of advice that might help," said the unbuilder. "Be still."

"Be still? What is that supposed to mean? Can you give me a hint?"

"No."

"Why not?" demanded the carpenter.

"Because this is one truth . . . "

"I have to discover for myself." The carpenter finished the sentence. "Fine." He was not amused.

Be still. The carpenter began to wonder what this might mean and how it might relate to his journey to the castle. At first it seemed at odds with the whole idea of the invitation and the journey. After all, how can you get anywhere by being still? He kept on walking. However, within a few days, he decided to stop and attempt to stay still in one place for a while. In doing so he discovered that there was more to being still than simply stopping.

At first he had to confront the thought that he must get moving, that he should be someplace other than where he was. Then he noticed that even when he wasn't walking, inside he was still moving. Inside he was still evaluating and judging himself and his surroundings. So the next thing he concentrated on was accepting what was in him and around him and resisting the urge to fiddle excessively with everything. It didn't help that there was a beautiful stand of trees nearby that were perfect for the kind of house he needed right then.

But as each temptation, each self-criticism, and each little bit of unsettledness arose, he concentrated on wrapping *be still* around it. This was how he greeted every thought and feeling. Soon he was able to set whatever it was aside and wait. Slowly it seemed as if one layer after another of desire for what he thought he needed was being gently peeled off to expose a more perfect layer of surrender and trust underneath. He stopped worrying about where he was and where he needed to be. He stopped worrying about how he would find his way to the castle and when he would finally get there.

At last one morning he looked up and saw something he had never seen before. In front of him on a distant hill was a great, gray stone wall. He looked to the left. The wall was there too. He continued to turn around and stare. The wall was all around him, in every direction, at the very limit of his sight. Suddenly he knew.

He knew that he was inside the courtyard of the castle. Everything he could see was inside. He hadn't seen it before because of what was inside him, not for any lack of travel. He smiled and looked for his companion, but the unbuilder was gone.

And in that moment he knew, as surely as he had ever known anything in his life, that he had come to the end of his journey as a carpenter . . . and the beginning of his journey as an unbuilder.

APPENDIX A

Group Exercises for Personal Formation

Here is a short selection of questions and processes designed to help groups anchor their conversations in Scripture and reflect on the purpose of church and each member's experiences of faith.

Questions for Helping People Reflect on Their Faith Stories

The following list of questions invites individuals to reflect on their own faith stories. Sharing aspects of our stories fosters understanding and builds trust among group members. Use these questions to begin meetings and group gatherings. Used over time, they help people heighten their awareness of God and increase their comfort and their ability in talking about spiritual matters with others.

1. When did you feel closest to God this week? When did you feel furthest away?

2. How did you first come to this church? What was your experience? Why do you stay?

3. What would be different for you if you weren't a Christian?

4. When did you first sense that God was real? What difference does that make for you today?

5. What are you most grateful for today? What are you least grateful for?

6. If this week has had a message to you from God hidden in it, what's the message?

7. If God is giving you a single word to guide you today, what's the word?

8. Whom did you meet this week who seemed like an agent of God?

9. Where did you see God at work this week?

10. What is the most fulfilling aspect of our congregation for you? What groups of people in our community might have a need for that?

A Bible Study on the Mission of Church

A. Read the following two passages aloud: Matthew 22:34–40 (the great commandment) and Matthew 28:16–20 (the great commission).

1. Although Matthew includes both in his gospel, some suggest that congregations are either "great commandment" churches (emphasizing love of God and neighbor) or "great commission" churches (emphasizing evangelism and disciple-making). Which category does your congregation tend to fall into? Which of the two are you most comfortable with? Why?

2. What, for you, are the challenging aspects of these passages?

3. How do you define "disciple"? How does a person become a disciple of Christ? What are the hallmarks of a disciple's life?

4. Matthew 28 points to baptism and teaching as the primary activities involved in "making" disciples. Why baptism and teaching? What is their purpose?

5. What does it mean for a congregation to love God? To love its neighbors as itself? How are the two related?

B. What Scriptures do you hold as foundational to your understanding of the purpose of church and of a congregation? How do they inform your thinking?

C. What is the good news that you have experienced, and how has it made a difference in your life? What motivates you to share that with others? When have you done that?

Using Scripture to Frame a Conversation

The following steps can be used as a way of anchoring a group as its members are preparing to discuss any topic that challenges people to think in fresh ways. This process is intended to help participants listen first to God and then to allow the insights that arise frame a time of talking and listening to each other. We recommend that groups participate in this kind of Scripture-framed conversation before gathering to make significant decisions.

Preparing and Claiming the Space
Gather in a circle so that people can see and hear each other. Place a Bible in the center as a symbol of God's presence and guidance.

Grounding Ourselves in God's Thoughts
Lectio divina is an ancient way of listening deeply to Scripture, with the "ear of our hearts" (St. Benedict). In reading Scripture this way, we imitate Elijah, who listened for the still, small voice of God (1 Kings 19:12). It helps us attune ourselves to the presence of God in Scripture.

To hear someone speak softly, we must learn to be quiet. The first step of this kind of Scripture reading is first to quiet down, to hear God's word to us. We are listening for the still, small voice of God that will speak to us personally—not loudly, but intimately. We read slowly, attentively, gently listening to hear a word or phrase that is God's word for us this day.

Any scriptural passage can be used as a focus. The following are only suggestions: Philippians 1:3–11, Romans 8:28–39, Romans 10:12–15, 1 Corinthians 12:12–26. If the topic is one on which the people are obviously divided, steer away from passages that would seem to support only one side of the conversation. Look instead for passages that speak to the entire group.

1. Have one person read the selected text slowly. Savor each portion of the reading, constantly listening for the "still, small voice" of a word or phrase that somehow says, "I am for you today." After the person has finished reading, be in silence with each other for one minute. Let the word or phrase that stood out for you sink into you. Repeat the word or words slowly and silently. Write it down, if you wish.

2. Now, have a second person read the same text slowly. (If his or her Bible is a different version, that is fine.) Once again, savor each portion of the reading, listening for the word or phrase that stands out for you. After the person has completed reading the passage, again be in silence for one minute, letting the word or phrase that stood out for you this time sink in. Again, write it down, if you wish.

3. Go around the circle and invite people to share the word or phrase in the passage that stood out most strongly for them. Imagine God using the words or phrases that God has given your group as a means of blessing, informing, and transforming into something holy the conversation you are about to have. You may wish to write the words people share on newsprint. Post the newsprint where people can see it during the conversation.

Talking with Each Other about Things that Matter to Us

If you do not have a topic selected beforehand, use the following question to surface one: "What's the most important conversation we could have with each other today?"

The conversation you are about to have is meant to be a space to speak and to listen, exploring both what you think and what others think about this topic. There is no decision to be made here, so you are freed from having to lobby or persuade. The goal is to be open—open in sharing your thoughts and feelings, and open to hearing the thoughts and feelings of others. The time may come when a decision will need to be made about this topic, but it is not today. The richer your conversation today, the wiser that decision will be when the time comes to make it.

End your time together with a minute of silence. Invite people once again to listen for the "still, small voice of God." What is the word or phrase, hymn, or Scripture passage that comes to them as a result of the conversation? Go around the circle again, asking participants to offer their word or phrase in benediction.

APPENDIX B

Processes to Help Surface
A Vision

The following exercises are creative ways to help a congregation get in touch with its unique essence or assist in surfacing a guiding vision. We've done these exercises with groups as small as twenty and as large as one hundred twenty. At the end of this appendix is a short list of other books that contain helpful tools and processes.

Most vision processes are best run by an outside facilitator, thus allowing all members of the congregation and the pastor to participate freely. An outside person is more likely to be perceived by participants as neutral and is less likely to have an emotional reaction to comments made by participants. A judicatory staff member or pastor or layperson with good facilitation skills from a neighboring congregation may be able to help in this way.

When you run an activity or process with a group, be sure to let people know what the purpose of the activity is. Create a setting and an atmosphere where people are comfortable and able to converse. Be sure to allow ample time.

Our Congregation's Essential Nature

Materials:

- sheets of newsprint
- markers for recording responses

1. Allow thirty to forty-five minutes for this first step. Instruct people to gather by the decade they became part of the congregation. For each group, supply one or two sheets of newsprint with the decade written across the top in large numerals. (Posting these on the wall or laying them on the tables ahead of time can help people find their group more easily. If a decade grouping contains more than fifteen people, consider having two groups for that decade.) Invite people to discuss and note on the newsprint group members' answers to the following questions:

   - What made the congregation unique in that time?
   - What about the congregation did you fall in love with?
   - What is the difference the congregation has made in your life?

2. Invite one person from each group to share briefly the essence of that group's discussion, posting the group's sheet of newsprint for the large group to see. In addition, invite someone from each group to share with the large group the difference the congregation has made in his or her life. *Allow ten minutes per group.*

3. Ask members of the large group to reflect on what they heard and what they can see on the sheets of newsprint.

- What were the common elements?
- What seems to be the essential nature of this congregation?

A Playful Visualization: "The Creature"

Materials:

- paper and a pencil or pen for each participant
- sheets of newsprint and markers for recording responses

Instruct people to sit in groups of five to eight, and give the following instructions:

1. Make sure you have a pencil and paper handy to take a few notes. Now, make yourself comfortable. This exercise makes creative use of metaphor to connect with the essence of a church or organization. Think of it as a playful, right-brain, intuitive exercise that will provide some additional information to lay alongside the harder data we will be gathering about congregation. Take a few deep breaths and close your eyes. As you breathe, feel your mind emptying and your body relaxing.

2. We're going to be thinking about this congregation. There are many churches in this world and in this city, some older, some younger. Among them is *(name of the congregation)*. It has been in existence for *(number of)* years and has somewhere in the neighborhood of *(number of)* members. I want you to use your imagination and let yourself imagine *(name of congregation)* as if it were a living breathing entity: a dynamic, shifting organism with a life of its own. Because you are part of that entity, you have your own experience of it.

3. In your mind's eye, let yourself connect with that living system called *(name of congregation)*. If it were a real or an imaginary creature, what would it be? *(Pause.)* Now return to your imagining . . . and imagine this creature moving through this community, this city. How does it move? What does it care about? Take a moment to jot down what comes to mind. *(Pause to let people jot down notes.)* This creature has magical abilities, so that when it comes in contact with people, they are changed. Whom does the creature seek out? What does the creature do? What change does the creature effect in people? Take a moment to anchor that picture in your mind, and jot down a few notes about what you saw. *(Again, pause to let people make notes.)*

Invite people to take turns in their table groups, telling each other about their "creature":

- What was the creature?

- What did you notice about it?

- What effect does the creature have on people?

Print the questions to guide their reflection on newsprint and post them. Ask the groups to select a recorder who will note people's answers and report them to the larger group. Allow twenty to thirty minutes, depending on the size of the groups.

Gather from the groups and record on newsprint:

- What creatures did people imagine?

- What effects did they have on people?

Allow five minutes per group.

Ask the large group to reflect on the following questions: What were the common themes you heard? What's energizing about what you just heard shared? What's frightening or disturbing?

Instruct the group: You've been given a glimpse of this animal called *(name of the church)* and have gotten a sense of its power and purpose. And you've heard others' perspectives—some similar to your own, some very different. Holding both, take three minutes in silence and complete the following sentence: "This congregation been put here to ————————.'"

Consider inviting people to write their sentences on pieces of paper that can then be posted for others to see. Invite those who wish to share to read their sentences aloud.

Creating a Picture of our Future

This process can be conducted by itself or as part of a larger workshop or retreat.

Materials:

- pictures and words cut from magazines
- large pieces of paper on which collages can be mounted
- glue
- a large empty stretch of wall, or an empty, movable chalk or whiteboard
- tape

Before the event, cut a variety of pictures and words from magazines. If you like, you can invite participants to bring pictures and words with them. Make sure that the words and pictures reflect a wide variety of people, situations, actions, and emotions—both positive and negative. For every person who will be present, have eight to ten words and pictures.

Before the event begins, lay out the pictures and words on tables on the side or back of the room. Instruct people to sit in groups of five to seven.

After an appropriate opening and prayer to help participants prepare themselves to listen for God's leading, inform participants they're going to be creating a picture that will give a glimpse of the future God has in mind for the congregation. Give participants the following instructions:

1. In silence, move to the tables and pick one picture that for you, today, represents God's picture of the future congregation. You may not know why that picture represents the future, but for some reason it does. It stands out to you, almost appearing to be highlighted. Imagine, as you're looking at them all, that the picture picks you. When you find your picture, bring it back to your seat and sit down, holding the silence.

2. Once people have selected their pictures, instruct them: Look at the picture you've selected. Still in silence and ask yourself: What is it about the picture that speaks to me? What aspect of my hope or God's hope for our congregation might it represent? Give people two to three minutes for this reflection.

3. This next part you'll do in your groups. One at a time, show the group your picture, without saying anything about it.

Group, your job is to notice in silence your assumptions about what you think that picture means to the person who is showing it to you. Then you'll go around the table and share your assumptions. "I assume you picked this picture because . . . "

Person who's sharing, your job is to listen and then, when everyone has shared, tell them why you picked it out. "Actually, this represents . . ." Give the groups about twenty minutes for this step. You may wish to add a break at the end. Have large pieces of paper and glue ready for the next step.

4. Still working in your groups, put your pictures together and create a collage. Once the collages are finished, have the groups reflect on the following questions:

- What stands out to you as you look at your collage?

- Are there colors, images, or themes that run through the various pictures? What are they? What do they suggest to you about the future congregation?

- Give your collage a name. Allow twenty to thirty minutes for this work.

5. Invite the groups one by one to hang their collages on the empty wall or chalkboard, and to share with the other groups their collage's name and main themes. Once all the groups have posted their collages, forming one large collage, ask the entire group to approach the wall and look for common themes.

- What stands out to you as you look at our large group collage?

- What themes do you see repeated?

- If this is a glimpse of God's vision for our congregation, what is the difference God wants to make in us and through us?

- What are possible names for our grand collage?

What in the World Is God Doing?

This exercise can be held as an "event" or part of an event. It can also take place across a period of three to four weeks. Prepare a visible and easily accessible bulletin board, titling it "What in the World Is God Doing?" Invite congregation members to bring in and post photographs (that they've either taken or clipped from the newspaper), along with short articles that speak to them about what God is up to in the community around the church and in the world. (If this board is "created" as part of an event, participants will need advance notice of what to bring.)

As vision work is being done by the congregation, this bulletin board can be used by various groups to reflect on what God is doing in the world beyond the church's doors. Helpful questions might include:

- What are the common elements in what people have posted?

- What seems to be touching the congregation's heart?

- What is it that God may be calling the congregation to take part in?

Other Helpful Resources for Vision Exercises

Branson, Mark Lau. *Memories, Hopes, and Conversations: Appreciative Inquiry and Congregational Change.* Herndon, Va.: Alban Institute, 2004.

Oswald, Roy M., and Robert E. Friedrich, Jr. *Discerning Your Congregation's Future: A Strategic and Spiritual Approach.* Herndon, Va.: Alban Institute, 1996.

Rendle, Gil, and Alice Mann. *Holy Conversations: Strategic Planning as a Spiritual Practice for Congregations.* Herndon, Va.: Alban Institute, 2003.

APPENDIX C

Powerful Questions

Questions direct people's attention to a particular topic. Powerful questions generate curiosity and open the door to dialogue and discovery. They spur new lines of thinking and lead to fresh insights. Albert Einstein is reported to have said, "If I had an hour to solve a problem and my life depended on the solution, I would spend the first fifty-five minutes determining the proper question to ask, for once I knew the proper question, I could solve the problem in less than five minutes."

Figuring out the right question to ask is a fundamental skill for congregational renewal. Questions are powerful when they help people surface and articulate what's important to them, when they help people gain fresh perspectives on old or existing situations, when they lead to "aha's" not only for the individual but for the gathered group. Powerful questions invite people to move beyond the surface of a subject and to explore more deeply.

This book is filled with questions designed to help people think about and discuss important aspects of congregational renewal. We've gathered some of them here and sorted them into categories. In general, when trying to ask a powerful question, avoid those that can be answered yes or no. Don't ask someone a question to which you already know the answer. Powerful questions should generate "aha's" on the part of the person asking the question, too.

Questions for Reflecting on the Purpose and Mission of the Church

- What's the fundamental purpose of the church? What difference is a congregation supposed to make in the lives of its members and in its surrounding community?

- What scriptures are foundational to our understanding of what a congregation is supposed to be and do? What are the unique denominational understandings of our work?

- What does it mean to be spiritual? What difference do spiritual practices make?

- What does it mean to be a follower of Jesus? How does someone become one? What helps a person grow as one?

Questions for Reflecting on the Congregation's Purpose and God's Vision for It

- How is God active in the world today? What difference does God envision the church making in the world? What role does God see individual faith communities playing?

- What is the purpose of *our* congregation in God's eyes? What difference are we supposed to be making in our own and others' lives? What's our mission?

- Who are we? Who is our neighbor? Why are we here? What does God want for this community and the people in it? How might God want to work through us to achieve that?

- Recall a moment when you experienced this congregation really "being church." What would be happening in the congregation if that were the norm?

- Whom does God want us to see? What is God's dream for those people?

- What does God want to do through us?

- Recall an instance in your current or a previous congregation's past when it listened for, discerned, and responded to God's calling. What was that experience like?

- If God wrote our congregation a letter, what would it say? What would we be commended for? What would God name as areas of needed growth?

Questions That Help Groups Do Their Work

- What is the ultimate aim we're trying to achieve? How will we know when we've accomplished that?

- What "baby step" would move us one step closer to our goal? How does taking this step serve our long-term aim?

When Stuck

- What's important to the congregation about this issue we're wrestling with? What's important to God about it? What's most important for us to keep in mind right now? Is there something about the way we're working together that's getting in our way? What do we each sense God's word might be to us to be right now?

When Assessing Current Reality

- Who lives in our area?

- What have been the changes over the past ten years? What changes are projected for the next ten?

- What are the primary challenges faced by the community right now?

- How does it feel to be part of this congregation? What's the mood on Sunday morning? What is it like to serve on committees here? What gets said in the parking lot that doesn't get said within the walls of the church?

- What do members say is the difference the congregation makes in their lives?

- What are the arenas where spiritual and faith formation are intentionally nurtured?

- How are business and other group meetings supporting the formation of the participants?

- How much is God a felt presence in our congregation? How do we introduce people to the teachings and practices of Christianity? How do we support existing disciples in their ongoing development?

RESOURCES FOR FURTHER EXPLORATION

Theoretical Foundations

These books explore more deeply the theory underlying the three phases of renewal, what is needed from leadership, the basics of dialogue, and the essential steps in creating.

Avery, William O., and Beth Ann Gaede. *If This Is the Way the World Works: Science, Congregations, and Leadership.* Herndon, Va.: Alban Institute, 2007.

Day, Katie. *Difficult Conversations: Taking Risks, Acting with Integrity.* Herndon, Va.: Alban Institute, 2001.

Fritz, Robert. *The Path of Least Resistance for Managers: Designing Organizations to Succeed.* San Francisco: Berrett-Koehler, 1999.

Heifetz, Ronald A., and Marty Linsky. *Leadership on the Line: Staying Alive through the Dangers of Leading.* Boston: Harvard Business School Press, 2002.

Hurst, David K. *Crisis and Renewal: Meeting the Challenge of Organizational Change.* Boston: Harvard Business School Press, 2002.

Johnson, Barry. *Polarity Management: Identifying and Managing Unsolvable Problems.* Amherst, Mass.: HRD Press, 1992.

Rogers, Everett M. *Diffusion of Innovations.* New York: Free Press, 2003.

Roxburgh, Alan J., and Fred Romanuk. *The Missional Leader: Equipping Your Church to Reach a Changing World.* San Francisco: Jossey-Bass, 2006.

Sellon, Mary K., Daniel P. Smith, and Gail E. Grossman. *Redeveloping the Congregation: A How-to for Lasting Change.* Herndon, Va.: Alban Institute, 2002.

Senge, Peter, C. Otto Scharmer, Joseph Jaworski, and Betty Sue Flowers. *Presence: Human Purpose and the Field of the Future.* Cambridge, Mass.: Society for Organizational Learning, 2004.

Books on Congregational Renewal for Group Study and Discussion

The following books are well suited for small groups that want to read and discuss a book on congregational renewal. They offer helpful insights and provoke lively discussion.

Bass, Diana Butler. *The Practicing Congregation: Imagining a New Old Church.* Herndon, Va.: Alban Institute, 2004.

Daniel, Lillian. *Tell It Like It Is: Reclaiming the Practice of Testimony.* Herndon, Va.: Alban Institute, 2005.

Hamilton, Adam. *Leading Beyond the Walls: Developing Congregations with a Heart for the Unchurched.* Nashville: Abingdon, 2002.

Harnish, James A. *You Only Have to Die: Leading Your Congregation to New Life.* Nashville: Abingdon, 2004.

Jones, Jeffrey D. *Traveling Together: A Guide for Disciple-Making Congregations*. Herndon, Va.: Alban Institute, 2005.

Schnase, Robert. *Five Practices of Fruitful Congregations*. Nashville: Abingdon, 2007.

Standish, Graham. *Becoming a Blessed Church: Forming a Church of Spiritual Purpose, Presence, and Power*. Herndon, Va.: Alban Institute, 2006.

Resources for Individual and Group Formation

These books provide practical tools and exercises for spiritual formation, group process, and team building.

Blythe, Teresa. *50 Ways to Pray: Practices from Many Traditions and Times*. Nashville: Abingdon, 2006.

Branson, Mark Lau. *Memories, Hopes, and Conversations: Appreciative Inquiry and Congregational Change*. Herndon, Va.: Alban Institute, 2004.

Bunker, Barbara Benedict, and Billie T. Alban. *The Handbook of Large Group Methods: Creating Systemic Change in Organizations and Communities*. San Francisco: John Wiley & Sons, 2006.

Cain, Jim, and Tom Smith. *The Book of Raccoon Circles*. Dubuque, Iowa: Kendall/Hunt Publishers, 2007.

Mead, Loren B., and Billie T. Alban. *Creating the Future Together: Methods to Inspire Your Whole Faith Community*. Herndon, Va.: Alban Institute, 2008.

Melander, Rochelle, and Harold Eppley. *Growing Together: Spiritual Exercises for Church Committees*. Minneapolis: Augsburg Fortress, 1998.

Pickering, Sue. *Creative Ideas for Quiet Days.* London: Canterbury Press, 2006.

Rendle, Gil, and Alice Mann. *Holy Conversations: Strategic Planning as a Spiritual Practice for Congregations.* Herndon, Va.: Alban Institute, 2003.

Sellon, Mary K., and Daniel P. Smith. *Practicing Right Relationship: Skills for Deepening Purpose, Finding Fulfillment, and Increasing Effectiveness in Your Congregation.* Herndon, Va.: Alban Institute, 2005.

Snow, Luther. *The Power of Asset Mapping: How Your Congregation Can Act on Its Gifts.* Herndon, Va.: Alban Institute, 2004.

Wheatley, Margaret J. *Turning to One Another: Simple Conversations to Restore Hope to the Future.* San Francisco: Barrett-Koehler, 2002.